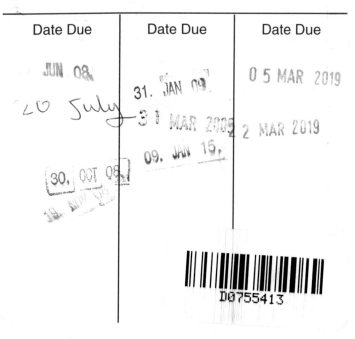

Blue Sky July
Nia Wyn

PENGUIN BOOKS

PENGUIN BOOKS

Published by the Penguin Group
Penguin Books Ltd, 80 Strand, London WC2R 0RL, England
Penguin Group (USA) Inc., 375 Hudson Street, New York, New York 10014, USA
Penguin Group (Canada), 90 Eglinton Avenue East, Suite 700, Toronto, Ontario, Canada M4P 2Y3
(a division of Pearson Penguin Canada Inc.)
Penguin Ireland, 25 St Stephen's Green, Dublin 2, Ireland (a division of Penguin Books Ltd)
Penguin Group (Australia), 250 Camberwell Road, Camberwell, Victoria 3124, Australia
(a division of Pearson Australia Group Pty Ltd)
Penguin Books India Pvt Ltd, 11 Community Centre, Panchsheel Park, New Delhi – 110 017, India
Penguin Group (NZ), 67 Apollo Drive, Rosedale, North Shore 0632, New Zealand
(a division of Pearson New Zealand Ltd)
Penguin Books (South Africa) (Pty) Ltd, 24 Sturdee Avenue,
Rosebank, Johannesburg 2196, South Africa

Penguin Books Ltd, Registered Offices: 80 Strand, London WC2R 0RL, England

www.penguin.com

First published by Seren, the book imprint
of Poetry Wales Press Ltd, www.seren-books.com 2007
Published in Penguin Books 2008
2

Printed in England by Clays Ltd, St Ives plc

ISBN: 978-0-141-03718-9

www.greenpenguin.co.uk

Love is not love which alters
when it alteration finds

William Shakespeare
Sonnet 116

For Joeski, with love

With thanks to my editor Penny Thomas, my family and friends, and everyone who has helped me on this journey

foreword

It's hard to imagine some journeys.
The kind that happen rarely,
to someone else,
and the kind the heart doesn't want to.

People often tell me that they can't imagine how it is for me.
Mothers especially.
They say they can't begin to understand the things I think and
feel and do; and that they don't know what, if anything, would
pull them through.
Perhaps it's impossible to imagine, unless it happens to you.

Because life can be changed in the split of a second, and
everything you think and feel and do changed with it,
changed completely,
changed within,
beyond all imagining.

This journey has a scale of its own,
a space between the lost and found,
that ends where it begins – inside me.

It's almost seven years ago now, the summer of '98.
And still, at times, it's like yesterday…

year one

(Summer '98)

WE'RE HAVING a baby, Alex and I. At the end of the summer. The doctor says that all is well, and my mother says life, as we know it, will never be the same again.

Time is in limbo in Market Road,
hanging around,
waiting.

When I left work and walked home through the city, I came in, put on the kettle and felt like I'd left my world behind. I sat for a while at the kitchen table; thoughts of the city, the paper and all its stories, dropping like litter about me.

Alex says I'll be back within the year, that newsprint's in my blood, but today, in my stripy top and dungarees, the whirl of headlines has unspun itself, leaving the simple equation of
boy or girl,
shining in its place.

The city collapses inwards,
and is stilled by a tiny heartbeat.

I am between worlds now I guess.

❖

On the window seat in the front bedroom, I look out on the stained glass arches of an old Welsh chapel, and up to a small patch of sky. I come here a lot now to talk to my big round belly, and to watch the mothers pass by.

When the sun raids the chapel in the late afternoon, it's like sitting in a rainbow.

Alex says it's exactly a year since we moved into this Victorian red-brick house in Market Road and next month, when the baby's born, the rose vine that clings around this window, will be full to bursting in a hundred, nameless shades of white.

We're growing together, the rose vine and me.
Almost ready, almost in bloom.

I think of Alex often when I'm here. At the picture desk in the *Western Mail*, shirtsleeves rolled up, black hair flopping in his eyes; at the coffee machine perhaps, making cheerful small talk with the typists; in the darkroom, watching light emerging out of shadow.

He calls from there, to say he misses seeing me across the newsroom. He says it suddenly feels real, having a baby, now we're apart.

In his lunch break today, Alex went to the Morgan Arcade and bought a smiling man in circus clothes who swings in a basket under a striped balloon.

❖

The weather's humid, close, like a calm before a storm. When I'm buying the paper and an orange ice-lolly, Sam in the corner shop says: 'It's gonna break. It's gonna rain, any day now!'

I've not been feeling well of late, just tired and thirsty, which the doctor calls 'quite normal', and Alex puts down to the heat-wave. We're in most evenings, him and I, pottering around half-naked together, playing U2 and watching the telly. Sometimes I sit at the piano and he plays guitar and we make up songs that make us laugh.

We often talk about this child to be, imagining some blue-eyed boy with rosy cheeks and golden hair, or some brown-eyed girl with jet-black curls in the tatty, patchwork dresses I've seen in the shops.

We imagine it will be just like the babies in the catalogues and the adverts on TV.

We can dream our lives away these evenings. The twilight hangs about for hours and the windows are awash with pinks and blues.

Last night Alex rigged up his old Decca player and we danced to the single he bought when he was eight: *I never promised you a rose garden*, by Lynn Anderson. He told me he bought it with his three bob pocket money at Woolworths in Reading after football practice one Saturday morning, and when he got home, his brothers called it poncy and said he should have bought Ziggy Stardust instead.

I love dancing with Alex.
He holds me as if I'm god-sent.

❖

In the study, the quietest room on the landing, we have filled four brown boxes to make room for the nursery. Odd bits and pieces, old camera parts, articles and magazines – stuff we don't need and can live without. Alex has filed all his photographs in one and I've thrown letters and diaries in another.

They sit side-by-side now,
in two little piles of word and light,
waiting to go up to the attic.

There's been a sense of *recueillie* in Market Road, a gathering in
of who we are, as we've idled away these hours, sorting through
photographs and flicking through diaries.

Alex says I've had a silver life between these pages – rites of
passage to be treasured, he says, like charms on a chain.

The sun rose behind a mountain, and fell in pieces through
horse-chestnut trees when I was young, and I followed its orbit,
in the middle of a brother, a sister and a big, white house called
The Moorings in a small, sleepy town by the sea.

Between these pages teachers tell me I have an unusual way of
seeing things, Keith Simpson says I look like Marianne Faithfull
and my school friend, Angela, says we'll be best friends forever.
Between these pages life is charmed, as Alex says. Silver.

Alex says life didn't really begin for him till he was twenty.
When he scraped together enough money driving a fork-lift
truck in a warehouse, to buy a second hand OM10 and do a
photography course. His very first pictures are of a log in the
steelworks, a bird on the wire – things he calls 'alien to their
environment', out of place.

He says his life changed the first time he understood light. He
was on a double-decker bus, travelling to college from Reading
to Henley when he suddenly saw the way it interrupted the trees,
and curved into shadow, and that life became another journey
altogether after that.

Alex says people rarely see the shadow; they forget that it's part
of the light.

❖

We have finished the nursery.

There are psychedelic rainbows on the wall, and a smiling man who swings in a small straw basket under a striped balloon.

Alex puts the boxes in the attic and, before we go to bed, we sit together for a while at the freshly-painted, old sash window.

Like two small children, watching the city lights die out.

❖❖❖

IF WE could only ever keep one feeling, from the whole of our lives, I'd choose this one. When heaven lands inside me.

Joe Alexander is born in hospital at 1.07pm on Saturday 29 August, two weeks early. He weighs six pounds and ten ounces, gets ten out of ten in his Apgar scores and has skin the colour of a pearl.

He is perfect.

Alex can't take his deep brown eyes off us.

Our son has jet-black hair, blue eyes and a cry that I've known longer than I've known myself. He is far more beautiful than we'd imagined.

We make our phone calls to family and friends. 'It's a boy,' we say, 'and all is well,' as smiling nurses breeze in and out, and the sun drops in through the window, spellbound.

It brings a new sense of time, this feeling, a new sense of love, a sense of the miracle.

Alex says it's as if we've been enlightened.

If I could keep one feeling, from the whole of my life, I'd choose this one.
This time, when just to be human feels divine, and nothing is wrong.

❖

It's the strangest time – a birth – for life to start falling apart.
Just like that!
The very next moment.

It's rare –
but it can happen.
And it happens to us.

It's so easy to slip between worlds, silver to black. There's
nothing in-between. Sometimes it's just a trip down the corridor
between heaven and hell.

It was 3.16pm when his skin turned a duskier shade of pearl and
a nurse stopped smiling. When she wheeled him off on a silver
trolley to intensive care,
and we chased her down the corridor,
as if she'd taken our insides away.

His skin is ashen,
his body shakes,
and his cry is changed so that even I don't know it now.

We sit at the edge of an incubator like children astonished, Alex
and I, and as doctors' summations merge with the irregular
bleeps like a shipping forecast we can't understand, we tell him
over and over how much

we love him.

So suddenly, it is all there is to say.

❖

There are two squares of glass in my room on the maternity
wing, one looking out on an ever-changing car park, the other
on to an ever-changing ward. When I look through this one, I see

all the perfect mothers and all the perfect babies and all the
perfection of unconfined joy.

I watch it as if it's my parallel world, and I feel like my arms have
been amputated.

He's still in intensive care and when I leave his bedside, I come
here and sit on my bed writing lists. 'Things to do,' I call them.
This is what I do when there's nothing to do, nothing that can be
done.

The doctor says that Joe keeps running out of sugar. He says he
doesn't need oxygen, blood or life support – just glucose. He says
he's big and strong and should be fine once he's stabilised. The
doctor says that I've been diabetic and that I should have had
treatment – it's just that 'unfortunately, it wasn't picked up,' for me.

Across the city Alex drives about in his silver car and thinks in fives.
It's the number one thing to do on the lists I make. To think in fives.
It's where we need Joe's blood sugars to be. Five is normal.

When Alex comes to visit me here he holds me in his arms and
says that all will be well. He tells me Joe will be fine and that we
will be closer than ever. He doesn't know that, when he goes, I
watch him walking back across the car park, and see him crying
in the car.

When the nurse comes to see me, she shoos the happy fat circles
of mothers away from the other side of the glass.

It's a stunning separation,
and the blurry moon spills over inside my belly,
setting hard as cake.

❖

I should be happy. We're going home today.
Everything's fine now. The doctor says so.
He's sure of it.
No damage.

Alex says it's all been just a bad, bad dream and that it's time to wake up. Time to be happy.

It's just that I don't feel it, sat in hospital, waiting.
Cases packed,
lipstick on,
and a baby in my arms that has a different cry.

❖

Alex makes a film of it. *September 14*, the label says: *Leaving hospital, Coming home.* It's a beautiful day and I am walking out of the hospital doors into bright light with Joe in a baggy blue suit in my arms. The sun is at its height; the shadows are long. My white top and jeans are over-exposed and there is a silvery haze around us. Alex says we look like angels.

Market Road is expecting us when we get home. The neighbours are on the doorstep and my mother has tied blue ribbons to the rose vine, which flutter like little sails in a sea of white. They all say they 'knew it would be fine at the end of the day'.

They give Joe teddy bears, love spoons and rattles, and take it in turns to hold him. They say he looks like Alex – that there's no trace of me anywhere.

This film ends as he's passed back to my arms. Everyone laughing and chatting and drinking champagne. I'm rocking him gently and smiling at the camera and, in the background, a few broken notes from a saxophone drift in through an open window.

I see Joe's arm is shaking slightly and I see mine move to calm it without even a glance.
I watch this film a lot these days. It seems to speak to me, though I'm not sure what it says.

❖

It's not like I imagined, coming home. The postman brings cards that say lovely things, and the phone never stops ringing with cheery hellos. Friends call round with gifts and compliments, but I'm not myself, and nor is Joe.

He doesn't sleep, he's fractious; and he arches back in my arms. It gets more and more difficult to feed him day by day.

Sometimes we have to dribble milk into his mouth with a syringe, like people do with newborn lambs.

The doctors still say there's nothing to worry about. They say he's passed his eight-week tests, has tracked an object and has smiled on time.

The health visitor comes and goes, nodding at me vacantly, and talking about colic.

She says I just have a touch of, what she calls, 'the baby blues'.

❖

The next-door neighbours say the saxophone player lives in Library Street, in a room in the student house that backs onto our square walled garden. They say he must study something else, because he can't even play a note in tune. I've grown accustomed to him though, these past few weeks, and when he starts his practice I open the French doors in the kitchen and feel comforted by his solitary battles.

When I first took Joe back to the hospital, I sat in a waiting room for hours until someone agreed to see us.

The doctors were still not concerned. They said it was natural for first-time mothers to be 'overly anxious' and that Joe looked fit enough and healthy. They just gave me some thickener for his milk.

Today, though, they seemed less sure. They said perhaps Joe wasn't 'thriving' quite as well as he should be, after all. They plan to run some tests.

I haven't told Alex. He struts about like he's ten feet tall and carries Joe's picture around in his wallet.

He must have shown the whole city by now.

He wants a party to celebrate.

I'm not sure what to say.

❖

They keep us in at the hospital, Joe and I. We have our own room on ward nine with a window, two cabinets, a chair and an aluminium cot with thick, steel bars. He lies inside it on a golden fleece, and I lie hunched beside him, stroking his arm and watching his eyelids flutter. The sun dissolves inside a cloud, and the radio plays a requiem for Carolyn, who visits her husband in ward 26 and wants him to know that he's loved.

The sky looks swollen,
as if it might break any minute.

Joe is not as he should be – everyone agrees now. At first they tried medicine, but it just made him worse – he started shaking and screaming.

His jet-black hair has fallen out.
He is barely responding.
The doctor says he's not sure Joe can see us now, and is concerned he might be fitting. He calls it flailing, the way Joe throws his arms out open wide and the nurse says it's not normal, the way Joe swallows, the way he arches back, the way he lifts his eyes.

These tests, these past few days have scanned and tipped and
turned and dismantled him – all of us – bit by bit. I lie here
wondering about him, this child of mine with bright blue eyes
and pale pink skin that is not normal. This child that once
tracked perfectly,
and now looks beyond me,
like someone communing with angels.

There is a brain scan booked for January.

I have called my father from the phone box in the corridor.
'It's the brain,' I told him, and then he couldn't speak and I
couldn't speak and we just stayed there like that, just hanging,
the line pressed up to his ear, and to mine.

I have twisted this door handle backwards and forwards
endlessly on the bright white clatter outside this room.
And I have now told Alex.

My parents have been to see me here. William, my brother,
came from Chester and Carol, my sister, flew from France, and
we've all sat here looking out at this sky.

It's the doctor that comes to see me now.

He tells me I should take Joe home until January, and try not to
worry. 'It's Christmas,' he says, and then looks in my eyes, puts
one arm round my shoulder and pulls my head awkwardly on to
his starched white heart.

The sky still looks swollen.
As if it might break any minute.
I don't know how it's holding on.

❖

My father has threaded tiny, white lights through the horse-chestnut trees. He says he's glad we've 'come home'. We've all 'come home' this Christmas: my brother's family, my sister's family, and Alex, Joe and me.

Life could pass for normal at The Moorings. Christmas, with all the trimmings. Dad sweeps snow off the drive, Santa comes with far too much; we all have babies. My brother says we shouldn't talk about the hospital. He says nothing's for certain until the scan, and we treat his words like gospel – it feels better this way.

We don't know how to deal with this. How would we?

When Alex first came to The Moorings he said it was like meeting the family in the yoghurt advert, all grown up. Summers have passed here with little ado, writing poems on the wide cream windowsill of my room looking out at the summerhouse, or looking back from the summerhouse at The Moorings, knee deep in flowers. William hitting a ball against the garage door, mum lazing on the terrace with Carol in *Rive Gauche* and yellow bikinis, dad mowing the lawns as the sun passed over, turning the French windows into glitter.

We can't deal with brain scans. We just try to keep things normal, positive, how they've always been, and how, somehow, they still will surely be.

Only now and again, we break the rules.

Like when the healer comes at six each evening, with her duffel coat and crystals, and holds Joe in the unsettled peace with tears in her eyes.

Like when we pray in dark corners.

Like when I sit with my mother in the kitchen, tying up paper prayers into scrolls with red ribbon, to bury in the garden,

as if the earth has a soul,
we can touch at such times.

❖

They leave the Christmas trees and decorations up in the children's centre long into January. The secretary says it helps morale because it's always such a bad time of year. The corridors are bright with tinsel, and on the wall in the waiting room there are colourful banners with the words Happy New Year splashed across them.

The world, as we know it, ends for us here, one clear, crisp Wednesday afternoon in January, with the words 'severe cerebral palsy'. The neurologist puts an x-ray on the wall, turns off the lights, and the moon blots out the sun in the middle of the day.

A total eclipse.

It means, the neurologist says, that the brain is damaged. The bit of brain connecting with the muscles. Sometimes, she says, it can mean a leg or an arm is affected, but sometimes, she says, depending on the spot, it's global.

We've been 'unlucky'. There are nine thousand or so muscles connecting to the brain, and it has affected every one of them. It means, the neurologist says, the most extreme disability.

She tells us plainly that Joe can't see. That in fact he'll never see, because the passageway is damaged. She says he'll never learn to walk,
to talk,
to do anything she can think of.
'He won't even know you,' she says into the dark.

To us, severe cerebral palsy means the world has ended.
And there is nothing left to hope for.

When we come back out into the waiting room, we sit amongst the tinsel again with Joe in our arms.
Alex says he wants 'to tear the fucking place down', but he doesn't.
We just sit here motionless, waiting for Joe's medicine,
and then we gather up our things in silence,
carry him out to the car,
and put our bags in the boot.

I drive us home, stopping for nappies at Tesco. I wander through the aisles and buy the ones with happy babies on a golden packet.

The check-out girl smiles when I go through the tills.
'New baby?' she says.

I can't speak.

Alex has been crying when I get back to the car.

❖

It's just as it was before we left for the children's centre. As if we haven't been away.
The good luck cards are still up on the mantlepiece and the blue ribbons I forgot to take down are still clinging to the rose tree, though the blue has faded in the rain.

As we walk back in, there is so little to show for what's happened.

A box of medicine,
a sleeping child,
and a note that says: 'A mother's prayer is the loudest prayer,'
all screwed up in my coat pocket.

❖❖❖

I DON'T know if Joe really does know us. We don't really know him. This is one of the questions my mother asks me on the phone each day, with the ubiquitous medical books on her knee. 'Do you think he has identified you as his mother?' And I say no, I can't be sure. It seems to make no difference whose arms he lies in. The hospital has put him on drugs for epilepsy and he lies between us motionless most of the time, like a distant dream.

We don't know him; we don't know each other; we don't know ourselves.

It's almost spring in Market Road and we've closed down, all of us.

Generally, we don't pick up the phone. People call to say they don't know what to say. We just watch the messages pile up on the answer phone, the distant voices of family and friends repeating over and over like a tired carousel, as if trying the fill the space between us.

We read the carefully considered cards that come, and put them up where the congratulations used to be. 'Be strong,' the new ones say, 'Our loving thoughts are with you.'

This is a private time. Our brand new boy does not respond, and we sit in his nursery amongst the toys that hold no interest, staring blankly at the smiling man in the striped balloon as time is cut

adrift.

Alex says I mustn't blame myself. The doctors have been clear on that – that I've done nothing wrong, that there's no-one to blame. But it doesn't feel that way. It feels like I've stolen from myself, without knowing how, without knowing why.

Our eyes barely meet now, the pain is so visible, and we circle each other like lonely planets, taking turns to sleep and comfort Joe's tiny body, seized by muscle cramps, in the night.

Sometimes Alex stands in the living room and stares at the photographs on the wall as if we're trapped inside them, as if we've been kidnapped into another world.

Sometimes, when Joe arches back in the night, he holds him with arms and hands turned upwards, like an offering to the gods.

One night Alex sits up all through, staring out at the flat, wet stars, and next morning he says: 'It's like death,' and slams the door. I watch him walk under the small shape of sky trapped between the chimney pots of Market Road and bury his head in the steering wheel of his silver car.

It is like a death.

I want to die.

❖

The physiotherapist says that 'perhaps it's best' that Joe won't know much. She says it's too severe when all the muscles are affected. She tells me to turn him sideways to pick him up, roll him over to give him a sense of movement, and lie him on his tummy to encourage him to lift his head. She says we have to help him find his 'bottom as a base'. She says 'they all' arch backwards.

The speech therapist says we must accept that he won't speak. His feeding problems are also severe. We use our tongues, lips, and muscles in our mouths with lightning speed to speak. It is, she says, 'a very complex matter' and, for him, 'it is impossible'.

The doctor at the eye clinic is a neat woman with swept-back hair and pink-coated lips. I cannot bear her. She says I must accept that he will never see, that I've just imagined he once used to. Mothers, she says, 'in my position,' often do.

She gives us so little time and has so little patience with my questions that I've started to dress up for our appointments. I wear my
navy-blue suit, my court-heeled shoes and I write things down
when I see her.
But I still feel unimportant,
slightly crazy.
I'm nothing like the girl I used to be.

At home, when I lie on the bed
and feel his feathered breath on my skin,
I can't relate these words to him.
He still looks perfect,
as innocent as the page,
before it is written.
That this sentence is trapped inside his lavender veins
is inconceivable to me.
'Unwrite it,' I beg the emptiness.
'Unwrite it.'

Alex says we shouldn't believe what we've been told. He says
they act like gods, these experts who have read Joe's destiny and
washed their hands of it. He says they're not omnipotent; that
they can't really know the future.

He comes home with tales of the unexpected, urban myths
about doctors getting it wrong, children raised from oblivion,
and he offers them to me like lifebelts.

He makes the tea, and sometimes takes us out to see healers,
who put their hands on Joe's head for ten minutes,
and charge twenty pounds.

❖

The gardens in Market Road are a mess this time of year. If I
stand in the corner of the back bedroom window, I can see all

the way along to the corner shop. The perfect lines of dry-stone walls and square back yards that look as if a storm's swept through.

Next door, the gnome has fallen, and the sign that says: 'Welcome Friends' is hanging loose from the holly tree. Christine and Ray have retired now. He has a new shed and the door is banging in the wind. Over the wall, Dave's long wooden benches are sodden and, over the wall from him, Derek's underpants drip-dry on a rotary line. Before he lost his mother, it span round with flowered dresses.

There's just a concrete yard with a skip that gets emptied every Friday at the corner shop, and beyond this Chapter, the red brick arts centre, where we'd watch late night movies, Alex and I, before Joe was born.

The need to heal him is overwhelming.

Beyond sense and reason.

Life is like an unrelenting wake behind this window as therapists queue up to try to rouse Joe's six-month-old body from its sleep and Alex says he doesn't know if we're brave to believe in such things or simply foolish. Despair, it seems, makes its own decisions and has needs beyond these thoughts.

From the French windows in the kitchen, I can't see beyond our garden. There is a slate-roofed shed, a naked tree and a dozen paper scrolls beneath the soil as the dry stone turns itself into an impossible wall of dreams.

❖

Sam at the corner shop tells me that in Pakistan, a household that has a disabled child is thought to be blessed.

He says it when I'm buying milk over the counter, Joe in a pale blue papoose on my chest.

He looks straight into my eyes and says: 'You've been so lucky, there isn't the medicine in Pakistan to save kids like him – you'd have lost him'.

Sam might have saved my life today.

I guess it's like that when you're dying;
you see a light
unless you don't.

As I walk back home, Sam's words pierce the cloud between my heart and the sun.

I hardly know Sam.
He barely knows me.

❖❖❖

WE DON'T go to the mother and baby clubs, Joe and me. I take him to special nursery out of town and sit in a line of grieving mothers, moving the limbs of our precious bundles to the rehearsed instruction of cheery volunteers.

I take him to the sensory rooms in the quiet corners of the city, where they play Mozart. The dolphins swim along the walls, the psychedelic bubbles float upward, and it feels as though we're breathing under water.

I take him to the oxygen tanks in Swansea where we lie in an echoey capsule under a poster of the Teletubbies and I sing nursery rhymes as I hold the black mask to his nose and mouth.

When my parents come to visit us, they wait patiently amongst the posters of brain-damaged children, and take it in turns to smile at us through the little round porthole.

I meet Jac here. He is with his grandmother in the tank next to mine. She says he's two and a half years old and bursting with life, but can't move his muscles. She says he lives in a dormer bungalow with his mum and dad in Llanelli and has shoals of silver fish on his bedroom wall.

Jac hadn't been able to say anything until one day his grandfather had asked him: 'Where's the sky Jac?' and he'd looked up; and, then he'd asked, 'Where's the ground?' and Jac had looked down. 'Right Jac,' his grandfather had said, 'Up is Yes, and down is No.'

Jac uses his eyes to say everything now.

❖

It's a particular time of day, around eight, when they call me. I'm lying in the bath and Alex brings in the phone and they say, 'Hi, it's me, how are yer?' just like they've been doing for years.

I know these voices intimately. I know their triumphs and their misdemeanours; all the details and dramas of their inextricable lives. They're part of my happiest times, Joanna and Julie, part of my memory of Newcastle University and, just like the dusty libraries, tin mornings and scatterings of pale, white butterflies around my bicycle wheels on the banks of the moonlit Tyne, they are part of all things silver. Joanna, with her bright red curls, her ra-ra skirts and problems, and Julie, when she liked The Cure and went out with a punk called Angel, are still part of the prosaic that I set my clock by.

Last year, when we all got pregnant, life seemed almost choreo-graphed for Joanna, Julie and I. We bobbed about in these bathtubs like synchronised swimmers, with babies floating in our tummies. Closer than ever.

It's as if we've lost our timing now Julie's had Freya,
Joanna's had Callum,
and I've had Joe.

I can't keep up with them.

Each time I try
it's like I'm treading water,
while they're powering past me,
doing butterfly.

The phone calls are not what they used to be as we fish about for words to connect such private bathtub heavens with such a private bathtub hell.

The phone calls in the bath have become excruciating.

❖

(Alpe d'Huez)

Through our window at L'Hotel Alpe d'Huez, the sun shines; the sky is blue and the snow is perfect.

We have a view of life skiing on soft white alps, and an open-air ice rink where the children skate round and round like music box dolls.

We have closed the curtains, Alex and I.

The whole family's come out to my sister's hotel for Easter, and they carry Joe round in their arms while we lie here in the dark and watch shit TV.

Sometimes they come up with little things to say to me.

My sister Carol says that we'll all stick together to make life the best it can be for Joe. Mum says she's still sure that one day he'll surprise us all.

When my brother William comes to my room, he says I should believe that nothing is impossible.

William says that on one of the motivation tapes he listens to at work, there is a speech by an American man whose child was born profoundly deaf, and that he taught him to hear by tapping on his spine.
I like it when he tells me that 'nothing is impossible'.

❖

(Market Road)

Back home we eat, we don't sleep, we see the therapists. Alex takes photographs of life in the city, and I watch the washing blow, and the clouds dry out.

I mix microelements into Joe's milk, do his exercises and make up his medicines in the kitchen.

When we sleep together in the afternoons his skin smells like candyfloss and his hair has grown back white as snow.

A girl from the paper came to check out the gossip this morning and stood on the doorstep asking me questions as her eyes crawled all over him. She asked how I was feeling.

'It's every mother's worst nightmare,' she said.

Joe's hand was shaking when she stood there and, for a moment, the briefest moment, I think I tried to hide it underneath my arm.

When I came back in and closed the door, I thought my heart would break.

My feelings are raw today, but there is one that cuts them to shreds.

He is not my nightmare.

He is my son.

❖

When the news comes on the radio it holds no meaning. When I look through the windows and the world passes by, it has no meaning.

Only Joe has meaning.
His skin, his smell, his breath
and I am lost in him.

The editor called to see how I was doing today, and I listened to the newsroom bustle, just streets away, as if it was a foreign country.

It's time for my quarterly column, he told me. I wrote two when I was pregnant, one about intensive care, and now the update's due. The editor said he'd understand if, things as they are, I wouldn't want to write it now. He said he wouldn't worry if he were me.

I wrote my column today.
I wrote it because
if Joe has severe cerebral palsy,
if he won't be normal,
and if there is no cure,
I want to explore his world with him.
I want to paint it brighter colours.
I want to turn the music up.
I want the world to know he's special,

beyond these words.

❖

(The Rescue Foundation, West Wales)

Gratia is ten years younger than me, but it doesn't matter. She grew up in a mansion in Chelsea that had its own cinema and yoga rooms; she doesn't speak or think or act like me, but it doesn't matter. We are next-door neighbours on this massage course this May and, when we talk I think we are as close as strangers can get – when they're still strangers.

Gratia does her sun salutations on a mat outside her door in the mornings, a motionless boy called Ioho Blue, looking skyward by her side. She tells me it takes nine hours a day to feed him and she is trying to build him up with ghee and Reiki. She says he has never responded, but she thinks he loves her and she loves him.

Sometimes we don't say anything at all, Gratia and I. We just sit together on her mat in the mornings,

massaging Joe and Ioho Blue
with lavender oil,
in perfectly balanced strokes.

❖

My column appeared in the paper this week.

My life splashed out across a page, my own picture looking back.

Of all the sob stories, in all the cities, in all the worlds, why did
ours have to be this one, I thought to myself as I put it in the bin.
I'd choose any over this one.

Alex says it was like reading a heart cut open, the stuff I wrote,
and that everyone's talking about it.

The phone has rung all day today. Friends on the paper plan to
do a cycle ride to raise money for therapies; people send website
addresses and the editor offers me a free press trip to Israel, as if
I've somehow merited a holier land.

I feel a wave of love and understanding.

Sometimes I'm in awe of Joe,
and the light he creates
out of such dark matter.

❖❖❖

MY BOOK has silver and gold threads entwined on the cover in the shape of a cradle. Alex bought it for me before Joe was born, 'to record his milestones'.

He has not had milestones.

These delicate pages are fenced in by my detailed analyses of healers, naturopaths and herbalists, and collect themselves now in notes, drawings and long passages of miniscule detail.

There is a diagram of a new massage technique I do, with arrows scribbled over the limbs and spine of a badly drawn baby, and a note to myself to repeat it twice daily. There is a chart of the purest fish oils, and a six-page list of the things I do to encourage his sight.

I record the litanies of the physiotherapist as if they're sacred.

At the front I have written that I believe Joe has been misdiagnosed, that something 'unknown, in some rare Amazonian flower', or some new approach will unlock him; that 'the world is full of undiscovered miracles'.

At the back are my lists of appointments and home-made healing routines, all covered in ticks before the end of the day.

Alex says the concentrated passages in this book are like the musings of a novice sorceress or an early religious order. He thinks it's my way of coping.

The doctor says I'm in denial.

He tells me it's pointless all the hoping I do, and that I'll save myself a lot of heartache, time and money when I start to accept that a cure is impossible.

❖

My family has clubbed together to buy me a laptop. They all send messages. When I turn it on it has a screen saver, which my brother has designed especially for us. 'Go for Gold Alex and Nia,' it says – 'Head up Joe'.

Joe can't hold his head up. It flops from side to side and back and forth when he tries, as if it's some highly complex balancing act requiring impossible strength and skill. He can't feel his muscles. We have been tapping them for weeks now, but there's no response, no connection to his brain. We tap, hoping his brain will eventually receive our messages. We tap from his arms to his legs, from his cheekbones to his toes.

The doctors say they've never heard of tapping. They also say there's no improvement; that nothing's changed, and all second opinions are exactly the same.

At Great Ormond Street, the opthamologist has wired him up to a computer to prove that his visual pathways don't work. She says I must accept now that it is quite impossible for him to see. Joanna was with me that day. She was showing Callum the bright and shiny toys in reception when I came out, and we walked back down the corridors to the main entrance together in silence. She drove us to Paddington station and waved us off, and I sat amongst the blank faces of commuters, tapping the muscles round his blue eyes, red lips and clenched white fists as we travelled back home.

I took him to the chapel across the road today. The place was draughty and empty and the sun was streaming in when I held him up to the fractured light of a stained glass window.

Today,
for the very first time,
I saw the way he seemed to prefer
to lift his face to the wind.

❖

The sun is weak, like a ghost of itself, but summer's here. Joe lies on his golden fleece by the French doors in the kitchen, listening to its music.

The neighbours potter, ice-cream vans pass, the saxophonist moves on to scales.

Alex and I have done a Reiki course and have certificates to channel healing this summer. I sit and watch him put his hands on Joe's head in the evenings. He says he really feels like he's doing something; but when I try I don't feel a thing.

We drive three times a week to see a cranial osteopath in Cirencester who charges £30 a session and holds Joe's head in his hands for eight minutes before we drive back home again. It takes one and a half hours there, and one and a half hours back and we squeeze it in between all the other appointments.

Alex drove home slowly today. He kept stopping to take calls on his mobile phone and then stopping just to look at the scenery. He stopped at a poppy field just before the motorway and decided to take photographs.

I carried Joe into the middle of them and held him up above my head.

Driving home, Alex said the light was sharper than usual, and that Joe and I had looked like one single snowdrop in a sea of fire.

We've lost weight, Alex and I. We noticed it tonight when we sat in our old Victorian bathtub, washing each other with Simple Soap as the water lapped around us.

I told him I wished we were on an island, him, Joe and me, far away from everything,
and he pulled me in tight
and said that we already were.

❖

We have his party at The Moorings. My mother bakes a cake, we sing Happy Birthday and I smile so hard my face hurts. Alex takes pictures in the garden, and I prop up Joe's head on my shoulder.

He takes dozens to get one that looks just right, just as I really want it – normal.

My school friend Angela comes, bringing champagne.
The birthday cards have glitter, music, and things to feel.
Joanna sends cot covers, home-made in the boldest stripes, to encourage his eyes.
My father buys a musical bear, which sings happy songs when you press its tummy and sits Joe on his knee, pressing it for him. My mother says he went out twice by himself to find something appropriate, something just right.

It's a year since Joe was born and the winter-white rooms of the hospital still feel like tombstones in the graveyard of my heart.

Before she goes to bed, my mother sits with me in the summer-house, watching the sun set. She says her pain is 'double', because she feels it for Joe and she feels it for me. She sits with me until the lights go out on Bishopswood Road and there is nothing to see but the empty black space between the stars.

My mother still can't believe that this has happened. She says we've always been so lucky, and that she thought I, in particular, had the luck of the gods. William had a rough start in hospital, Carol took life seriously but I had serendipity, she said, the like of which she'd never known.

Life just worked out for me without much effort on my part. Blessings fell like windfalls; boyfriends arrived like mail, exams were scraped through. I was the one she never worried for.

I still can't believe it either.
Joe and Alex, all tucked up in my childhood bedroom,
as I drain the dregs of the Moet,
and watch the sky break over the pale pink mountain.

year two

JOE IS a beautiful child. He transmits gentle epiphanies as I carry him around in my arms like a broken Buddha or a broken doll.

I walk with him every day as autumn steals the last of his first summer and the burnished leaves fall about our heads in Pontcanna Fields.

Nestled into my chest in his brown, furry coat, we look no different to the snuggled silhouettes of all the other mothers meandering away these mornings in the city's peeling parks, but we speak a different language in our skin. His fallen head rests on my heart and he knows its unsteady beat fading in and out as we pass the grey salty waters of the Taff, the quiet cathedral and the merry-go-round in Queen Street twirling the last rides of the holidays.

He gives the world an unbearable intensity.

His blindness gives me new eyes to see, new ears to listen to the languages of nesting birds and echoing arcades, new understanding.

Pain mingles with a profound sense of beauty. Carrying him makes everything burn brighter.

As we pass the running children who hold up their heads so easily, I realise miracles are so commonplace we barely recognise them anymore, and near the circles of mothers anxiously comparing milestones at the school gates, I see how we live in a time where normal is never enough,
and we are never full.

Joe gives me insights I could never have understood without him, and he gives me heartbreak.
To separate these two responses would be impossible.
He is equally beautiful and terrifying.

❖

When Gratia brings Ioho Blue to Market Road, she hangs crystals over their beds, and tells me we have wise old spirits in our arms.

She says it's probably the last time for their souls on this earth, and that we have been chosen to care for them.

I like to listen to Gratia and the mystical messages she brings me from her yoga trips to Egypt. We can hide away for days together in our own special dimension, imagining something good is in store for our baby boys. Imagining sometime, somewhere, something good will happen.

When Joanna and Julie come to visit, they watch Callum and Freya toddle about in the back garden, shouting and splashing in the puddles, while I massage Joe on the kitchen table,
behind them.

❖

Between the Menai Bridge in Anglesey and the Severn Bridge in Bristol, I pass through patchwork quilts of mountains, rivers, valleys, seas and streams. The night editor and the boys from the paper look like different men in their shorts and t-shirts, riding their bikes between the sea and sky.

My childhood friend Keith Simpson has organised houses and hostels, bunk beds and floors along this route, and friends turn up with bright sunny smiles in rainy Welsh towns. Julie drives one of the breakdown trucks and I drive the other, and we weave our way along, waving to each other as the boys stretch and sail and climb before us.

And the rain and the sun swap places.

Alex says sponsor sheets are dropping through the letterbox in Market Road covered with the signatures of people we've never met. He says there's a list of names from a school in France, an office in Chester, and the herb garden in Redcliffe Bay, Australia, grown by Auntie Rosie and her pensioner friends.

I think of this when I'm driving my truck
between these bridges,
watching people climb mountains,
and show depths
I never knew they had.

❖

The coffee table in the living room is full of clutter.

There is a book about cerebral palsy and the small rubber toothbrush that I use to massage the inside of Joe's mouth.

There's the deep red lipstick and sparkly wig I put on to try to get him to look at me, and the bright pink feather I use to coax open his clenched white fists.

There are the photographs of his first birthday. His eyes look slightly crossed. I hadn't realised.

There is the small brown bottle of the homeopathic pills I give him on the hour, a cloth to wipe up dribble, and my little gold and silver book where I've lodged a note to myself to call the physio, and ticked off the day's routines.

There is also the envelope from the hard-nosed newsman I used to sit by on the paper. He's sent me pages of carefully selected information about the RNIB, and buried in the black and white print is a line that says: 'blind children see with their hearts'.

Alex says there's no time or space for anything in this house anymore.

He says before Joe was born he used to put his feet up on this table, and there's nowhere to put his feet up now.

❖

There are so many of us, I had not known, and yet I know so many now. I meet them in the quieter corridors of hospitals, the Scope centres and the RNIB, these mothers who have kids like Joe, and who are, I guess, like me.

There was nothing to unite us before we got here, no age, no class or story, but now we're here we're all the same, circling these places like dislocated puppets as the therapists pull at our strings, sharing the stuff of our souls,
round the coffee machines.

We're ghosts of ourselves by the time we get here. A long way off the beaten track and, in each and every one of them, I see my own small reflection staring back.

It is another world, this network that collects us from the mainstream.

Behind closed curtains, behind closed doors
there is an unseen planet,
hidden away in society's pockets,
and slowly revolving at its core.

❖

(The Rescue Foundation, West Wales)

Gratia hasn't been invited back to The Rescue Foundation. The charity does not think Ioho Blue can benefit from its courses, so she sits at home in Brighton, wondering what to do. The rest of us have not had miracles but have all returned to this row of stone cottages, nonetheless, to try again.

A well-dressed woman at the centre says the course will help our muscle-tapping techniques and explain where we may be going wrong. She gives us each a photocopied book with new exercises to do, which we treat like the Holy Grail.

The mother next door, whose three-year-old son bangs his head on the wall eight to ten times a day, says nothing's really changed since she came before, but that she still has faith it will.

Sarah, two doors away, says her eight-year-old still rocks backwards and forwards and screams constantly, but this place is her last hope.

The girl who lives in the cottage at the end, tells me she'll have to give up her job as a psychologist if she doesn't cure her 'brain-damaged baby', and so she had no option but to come. She's having a breakdown, running in and out of the therapy sessions, instructing her husband to make notes and feed the baby, while she calls her office on her mobile phone.

When my mother comes to stay with me here she says this single row of stone cottages is the most desperate place on earth she's ever been.

When Joanna and Julie come, with their arms full of food and wine and healthy babies, they say they just can't believe that we're all here.

❖

The physiotherapy room at the hospital in Cardiff is large, white and sharp with morning. I lie on the floor with Joe and there is a wooden toy with bells and mirrors in between us, sparking the white light.

He doesn't reach out. He never does.

Two other children are waiting; one has a bowleg, the other has Down's. The wind undresses the trees in the window, the phone rings and stops again, and the receptionist reads a headline in *The Western Mail* that says: 'Life is better than ever'.

These appointments are gruelling affairs. I'm here almost daily, watching the portage teacher try to interest him, the physio roll him over and the speech therapist battle to coax out a word. She gives him a toy and takes it away again, saying: 'More, More, More, More, say More and you can have it back'. But he doesn't say or do anything, and she says she has nothing to work with, that there's 'no initiative'.

In Market Road, I write my journal and trawl the world-wide web as far as the borderline clinics in Mexico, where only the desperate go.

The neurologist won't reduce the drugs – I tell her I have a hunch he'd do better without them. But she says it's out of the question – ridiculous – that he'll always need them.
The doctor says that I'm depressed. He says maybe I should have another baby, but I don't want another baby.

I just want Joe.

Sometimes, in the afternoon, I send emails to William who sends them back in minutes from his office in Chester. Sometimes, in the dead of night, I send emails to Carol, who writes back next morning from her farmhouse in France, where the sun still shines and her three blond children dance about her like a snowstorm.

The sky is bruised in Market Road today.

I want to know my son.

The clouds are as black
as they come.

❖

I go to Israel in October. I cross the desert in a Land Rover, listening to the idle chit-chat of kitten-heeled beauty editors. I watch the Bedouin tents float by in the haze, and write a travel piece for the paper.

I lie naked in the Dead Sea as the sky turns maraschino.

I bury two prayers in the Wailing Wall in Jerusalem and pass the site where the Jews revere Solomon, and the Muslims say Mohammed ascended into heaven.

I watch the light fall on the cracks in the Via Dolorosa early in the morning.

I yearn for something to believe in.

I buy a tacky model of a Madonna and child in the Kasbah, and want to come home.

This sadness still swallows me
whole as the moon.

❖❖❖

THE CHAIR with belts and buckles arrives in November. It looks like something off Death Row.

I have to strap him in to feed him now, so we can sit face to face, but his head still falls to the side. 'Head up Joe,' I keep on saying. 'Come on now.'

Sometimes I throw a flowered tablecloth over this chair, but when Alex comes home he takes it off again.

He says I must accept that it is part of life now.

❖

Nothing much happens this winter. I take Joe to The Moorings and Alex stays in Cardiff to take pictures of children in their Christmas plays.

The papers are full of them – Mary and Jesus everywhere!

Millenniums swap over – it's the two-thousandth birthday of Christ – and the world has a party to celebrate. Seventy-five thousand queue up in the rain in Cardiff to leave the twentieth century with the Manic Street Preachers, and the rest of the world lights up the future.

Fireworks everywhere, like rainbows cracking into dust.

I watch them on telly with my mother. 'I can't see a future,' I tell her, and she hugs me like I'm a small girl and says something will come to help, she's sure of it.

Alex phones to wish me Happy New Year and we sob together outside our parents' houses in Reading and North Wales.

This winter we both need our mothers.

Some say Christ will return in the New Year. Thousands tread the bible-trails along the Sea of Galilee and queue up, just like him, to be baptised in the river Jordan.

Scientists call it a new age, an era of medical and technological breakthroughs with, as yet, unknown possibilities. They have discovered the blueprint of the human genome and predict they'll soon be able to cure the incurable.

I listen on and off, to those that say God is amongst us, and those that think they have become Him but, either way, there is still no miracle.

Nothing much happens. Against the neurologist's orders, I start to reduce Joe's drugs for epilepsy. I say I need to try – she says I'm mad. Alex tells me to follow my heart so we give Joe deer horn from a Chinese herbalist and tick off more hours singing echoey songs down in the oxygen tanks.

I light fires in the late afternoon, write my journal and read a book called *How to Save your Own Life.*

The corner shop closes for two weeks due to deaths in the family, the water pipes freeze, and the moon passes over the kitchen table.

❖

(Peto Institute, New Year)

Everything seems broken: the broken English of the stern Hungarian conductors and the broken spirit of mothers who bring their broken children here.

We stand in long rows at these therapy rooms, willing our children to crawl along the wooden plinths, and looking on helplessly as they strain and flap like dying fish.

Julie lives just streets from The Peto Institute in her pretty terraced house in Islington, as if somehow it was meant to be. Each morning, she drives round the long way to drop us off when she takes Freya to nursery and we all sit in the car singing songs and squealing as we go over the sleeping policemen.

Freya can walk, talk and ask intelligent questions now. She cuddles Joe in the back of the car as if she is his grandmother.

These London mornings have the shape of damp fog – I feel them in my bones.

Each day here I discover more multitudes of things he'll never do; the complicated steps and fine motor skills that must be mastered when action is no longer automatic. What perfectly co-ordinated muscle groups it takes to feed ourselves, brush our hair or say a word. There's so much I haven't thought about before; so much I take for granted, so many millions of dots to join back up when instinct breaks down.

At night, we stay up late, Julie and I, drinking red wine. Sometimes she cries; sometimes she tries to take my mind off things. She talks a lot about the people that we used to be. The house we shared in London in our twenties and the long-lost men that graced it. There was the beautiful boy from the bookshop and the guy that rode a unicycle in white bloomers and looked like Jesus Christ. There was the millionaire businessman in his navy blue suit and Jag, and the bloke across the road who drank whisky, played backgammon, and liked to dress up in the afternoons.

I don't sleep at all at Julie's house. When she goes to bed I lie awake in her red bedroom, looking at the walls – at her tatty

Peruvian bags and Che Guevara poster,
at her shelf with neatly labelled boxes,
at her neatly labelled life.

The moon looks like the one in Mary Poppins when it comes to
this window,
and, before I know it,
it's morning,
and time to go back over the bumps again.

❖

The therapies are ridiculous, out of control. Alex goes freelance
to help me.
The patterning needs two, several times a day, and several times
a day, between jobs, he races home to pattern with me.

We lie Joe on a table and move his arms and legs in the patterns
babies use to crawl. Over and over again, moving arms and legs
the way that babies crawl.

Sometimes we sing Joe nursery rhymes, sometimes we tell him
stories, willing him into our world. He rarely shows interest, but
we think he smiles more these days, that he's more with us
perhaps, more in his body. We have noticed his arm doesn't
shake anymore.

Judit arrives at 7.30 on the dot each morning, our private Peto-
trained conductor, who charges £15 an hour and has her own
key. She comes into our room and lifts him out of our bed. We
roll towards each other, Alex and I, as she carries him through to
the front, opens the blinds and the light stretches down the
landing and over the wooden floors into our room.

We listen as we lie here and can now predict her every line. As
she lifts his arms above his shoulders she will say: 'Open your
hand Joe, hold the glitter stick'. As she moves the purple puppet

close to his eyes, she will say: 'Look at it Joe, look at it, lift your head up'. When she is moving his arm in a circle she will sing, 'round and round the wheels go round, round and round the corn is ground'.

Judit ends her strict routine with a butterfly kiss, putting her eyelash to his cheek and fluttering it.

It is 8.30 now. She will offer to do the early patterning session with one of us before she leaves.
I tick it off my list,
as she disappears into the day,
like some keeper of dreams.

❖

(18 months)

The neurologist says it doesn't mean much in the grand scheme of things, but this small scrap of paper that she holds in her hand means everything to us.

It says there is no trace of epilepsy in Joe's EEG tests.

It has the words: 'Brainwaves – Normal'.

This small scrap of paper says there's no need for the drugs now, after all.

Perhaps the neurologist just doesn't know what to say.

Alex says we've been wise to follow our hearts.

❖

It is spring. I can see it and feel it, and I know Joe can feel it too.

The daffodils look like paths of sunlight all about the hospital, and the trees are already making leaves outside the physiotherapy window.

Today, when I lay on the floor with him, the wooden toy with bells and mirrors in between us sparking the light, his left arm slowly inched forward,
and made contact for the very first time.

I sent an email to my family and friends.

'Joe reached out,' it said. 'He has managed to move the muscles in his left arm.'

He has a will.

There is a spark.

❖❖❖

WE BUILD the light room where the nursery used to be. The life-less toys look just as they did two years ago, blank and undiscovered, no favourites as I pack them back up into boxes. The words 'Welcome home little Joe,' have still not been rubbed off the blackboard when the man in the striped balloon comes down.

It's as if nothing's happened here, as if time has been still.

I put black bin bags on the window and I lie him under the 240 watt bulb that I switch on and off at five second intervals for three minutes, five times a day.

'Look at the light Joe,' I say,
'look at the light.'

Then I offer a wordless world to his eyes.

Pictures of the teddy bears and teapots Joanna has painted for him in fluorescent ink, green plastic stars and flashing Christmas tree lights – anything lurid, everything bright.

Sometimes I use a torch and imagine the passageways between his eye and brain are listening to my voice.

'Touch the light,' I whisper,
'touch it.'

The light room is a kind of meditation for me. I have the barest communion with myself here. The statements of 'No Visual Response' and, 'It Is Impossible,' echoing through my mind, as I turn the light

On,
…and off,
…and off
…and on.

❖

We talk on the phone most days now, Sue and me. Alex calls her my new best friend and tells me I can't live without her.

Sue says we have to work things out for ourselves, mothers like us, and she stays up all night scrutinising the world's sparse offerings of research papers on cerebral palsy, piecing together her own home-spun prescriptions.

Sue says she feels the doctors just aren't interested and that it's up to us mothers to find the answer now.

Before Sue had Marchant, she was a doctor of chemistry at the university in Bristol, but now she devotes her life to her four-year-old son who cannot move his muscles. Her salubrious address is like a shrine to him. He has a train that travels the entire downstairs on a sensor wire under the linoleum floors, a full-sized trampoline in his bedroom and a slide from the window into the sunken garden. At night he falls asleep under the transfer she has painted on his wall, an angel in gold ink, tall and wide,
the words 'Where did you find the wings to fly?'
written at its right-hand side.

Sue encourages me to keep going. She says we can make a difference, no matter what we're told. She says Marchant is able to speak now with a board of letters if she supports his hand, and that he taps out all kinds of things upon it, sometimes about Man U or Bristol City, sometimes about God. She says he likes to go out to the café bars in Clifton, and when she takes him in the afternoon, she pushes him along the pavements in a bright red walking frame on wheels.

She hasn't even bought a wheelchair.

Sue knows everything there is to know about therapies and equipment. She sends me special toys and catalogues from overseas.

Alex says I talk more to Sue than I do him these days.

He complains he can't get a look in,
and just can't reach me anymore.

❖

(May weekend, Paris)

We can hear the bells of Notre Dame in our flat in Paris. They
wake us in the morning, Joanna, then Julie, then me.

In the daytime we walk past the Pompidou Centre, the Eiffel
Tower and over the bridge where Diana died.

We don't talk about children.

We pass a carnival in the Latin Quarter, a Ferris wheel and an
old-fashioned merry-go-round in the park.

I wish I wasn't depressed,
in one of the most beautiful cities in the world.

❖

(Market Road)

The house is upside down.

The front room is Joe's therapy space, the nursery a light room
and our bedroom is cluttered with equipment. Joe still sleeps
between us.

Love revolves around the patterning table, and hobbies gather
dust, like signs of a past life that has lost all meaning.

Alex says the red brick art centre in Market Road has had dozens
of good films this year, and we haven't seen one.

He says he misses jobs, dashing back and forth across the city to pattern with me. He says he misses life.

We're like zealots with our rituals and light room this two-thousandth midsummer. Like the early Greeks, who built monuments to gods they didn't know, but hoped would come one day.
They're our testament to hope, whatever the odds against it, and they keep us going. I think, without them, we would fall apart.

My cousin Ffion died this week. She was only twenty-eight. I watched her coffin, covered in sunflowers, carried in from the light to the dark chapel as we sang the Welsh hymns and I remembered us as two small girls, dreaming about how life would work out.

Her mother said it is the greatest loss.

Today I feel so lucky to hold Joe in my arms,
and feel his heartbeat next to mine.

❖

My dad says I'm like a small industry arriving at The Moorings this August.

I've brought Judit and Joe, mats and bottles, two special chairs and a 240-watt bulb.

We pattern endlessly and turn the back-bedroom window bin-bag black.

Joe turns two.

Alex comes for his birthday, but has to get back.

❖

*(Malagny at the
end of summer)*

From my balcony, the tiny French village of Malagny looks like an island in a sea of colza fields.

It's like a dream here. The enchanting white farmhouse with its faded blue shutters, the wooden table in the orchard, and Joe in the brown-skinned arms of his cousins. I can see his fallen head as he swings under the heart-shaped leaves of the Katalpa tree and hear the merry cries of 'Bravo' when he lifts it, momentarily, to the delight of Aurelia, Ambra and Teo who dance in circles about him.

We pattern outside in the sun most mornings, as the village children walk past and watch us through the gates. Alex sings French nursery rhymes to keep the time and make us laugh.

Sometimes, my sister's friend Prisca brings her horse down the lane, and takes us round the village on his bare back. We go past the little fountain, past the old school, under the walnut trees and home again. It's the highlight of Joe's day, listening out for the clippety-clops to come.

There's a healer in Chavenoz, an old man who villagers say can perform miracles.

He holds Joe silently in his dark study, which looks out on fields of corn. He says he thinks he'll walk at the age of three and be a *civilisé* – an educated man.
My sister puts one hundred francs in a tin on the table when we leave, and says she believes in miracles.

Today, after lunch, Alex and I patterned him on the bed in the cool air of our attic room, moving arms and legs, as the sun fell in streaks through the weather-beaten shutters.

Alex read a book when we'd finished and I put Joe to bed.
I sat for a while, watching him drift into sleep, and when I moved
to go, without making a sound he slowly, stiffly, raised one arm
and then the other, around my neck…
and hugged me.

I never knew a hug could mean so much.

Joe knows his mother now.
He feels my love.

It's like a healing has begun.

year three

WE HAVE developed an extraordinary closeness, Joe and me. Our worlds are inextricable.

My arms move for him, my eyes see for him; I bring the world to him.

We are constantly swapping bodies: using each other. His clenched and knotted muscles imprison him outside my arms, and my fears for him paralyse me outside his.

When I'm despairing, I always turn to him,
to what I can touch and hold.
We are one.
Quite inseparable.

Alex says I've created a cocoon around us here in Market Road, weaving the threads of our daily therapies so tightly around our lives that the whole world has disappeared.

He says I've lost sight of who I am and what is normal, though sometimes I catch glimpses through the windows,
through the glass,
life rushing,
whirling,
past.

We've lost an intimacy, Alex and I. We're out of balance. He says I've disappeared into a world that he can't access and that I only think of Joe these days. He says he feels left out, as if he's running ahead or falling behind, as if we're journeying without him.

Alex says there's no love anymore,
no life,
no love life.

Joe is my love life now. I can't take my mind off him. I wonder what his world is like, what he's thinking as he lies under the light, or as we hover above him, patterning away.

I wonder how things appear when they can't be seen and what he experiences when we tap his muscles.

I wonder what he feels,
and what he believes,
when he lies in my arms.

Alex says we should go out together one evening, just us two, but there's always far too much to do.

❖

When Alex takes Joe out, he carries him high up on his shoulders. He takes him to see all his friends, and even on his photo-shoots of businessmen in the city.

He says after all the battles we've fought to bring Joe closer to our world; we're going to make damn sure he's part of it. He says he's proud to show him off.

I wish I were more like Alex.

Now I can't amble through the parks and passers-by unnoticed,

I see our reflection everywhere. I see how no-one ruffles his hair
the way they do to other children.
I see them look the other way,
I see them stare.

In a world full of eyes, I can see how some strangers love and
some strangers hate without even knowing it themselves.

At times I see myself in them.
At times I see myself stare back,
and wonder how I ever got to be at war with my world.

Occasionally, I see myself in shop windows, secretly rearranging
his awkward body on my hip, adjusting my posture so that his
head will look more upright on my arm. Even I am self-
conscious in his presence.

Society separates us. It seems to fear the vulnerable.

In general there are two trains of thought regarding disability.
Either it's an overwhelming tragedy, a life to be lived in suffering
and frustration, or – where nothing else can be blamed – it's
sinful. The England soccer manager has just resigned after his
declaration that disabled people are paying for deeds in former
lives and, in Cardiff, there is a commotion when some youths
stand outside a school for special needs, shouting 'sinners', at
the children wheeled onto the buses.

Doctors call it a question of statistics; one in forty children are
severely disabled for life, they say, and often there's no rhyme or
reason. Friends say bad things happen to good people – life's a
bitch! Others say God chooses special parents for special children. Alex laughs when he hears this one. He says he still
remembers his press trip to the orphanages in Minsk, where
thousands of special children lay abandoned in iron cots, staring
at the ceiling all day long.

There are 8.6 million disabled people in Britain and at least 610 million disabled people worldwide. Fifteen to twenty per cent of every country's population are affected and yet the views and words society uses to define them still have the power to single them out.

They're all 'dis' words – 'disabled, dystonic, diseased' – words that set them apart, at best turning them into beggars – handi(n)capped – and at worst negating them as people – invalid!

These words steal humanity,
reflecting views like those towards Jews in the Holocaust, and those towards 'blacks'
for a century.

Alex says people think that Joe is beautiful, and that he doesn't give a damn what they think anyway.

I think he's beautiful too, but I wish I could be more like Alex.

❖

Sometimes when we pattern, moving arms and legs in perfect choreography, singing songs with faultless timing, we're like one, Alex and me. Dashing in and out of light rooms, passing Joe between us, ticking off exercises on the very same list.

We share one heart; we share one will.

And sometimes we're such separated souls. When he wants the radio and I want peace. When I want to explore Joe's condition from every angle and he wants to talk about something else. He says I never do that any more.

There are times we only seem to see the gaps in each other.

Times we take our bodies off at night, and hang them by the bed.

Alex says there's nothing worse than being with someone you love and watching the distance grow between you.

Sometimes I think distance and closeness are the very same thing.

❖

The counsellor in the city says our grief is 'tangible', but I know that he has no idea how it feels.

When we saw him, he asked if we'd mind being watched behind his two-way mirror for learning purposes. He had freshly combed brown hair, and had just had a holiday with his wife and kids in Ireland, which he said was 'simply wonderful'.

We were worlds apart.

The counsellor says we have shrunk our grief into our ever-increasing therapies, and that somewhere in the process we have shrunk ourselves. He says we should make a list to plan in time to be together, but our walls are covered in lists. There's no space left.

It's too late to piece back together what is falling apart. Perhaps I don't want to deep down. Perhaps there just isn't the time.

The counsellor told us to pull the two soft, leather armchairs closer together when we talked, but we both looked out through the window, Alex and I.

Alex said he wanted order, and that his life and his home were in chaos, that he missed jobs racing home to pattern with me and had fallen a month behind on invoicing.

Alex said he felt damned if we continued Joe's therapies, and damned if we didn't. He said it was like we'd been given 'a life sentence', with no explanation of what we'd done to deserve it.

Alex said he wanted to be loved, the way he used to feel loved.

It feels misty inside me. I think it might stay this way forever.

I am losing him and feel I have no choice.

The counsellor says I do have a choice. He says it's my choice to fight Joe's odds, whatever the cost; a choice perhaps most people wouldn't take. He says it might not seem to me like I have a choice, but it is my choice all the same.

He says clever things, the counsellor. I think he knows a lot about grief; but I don't think he's ever felt it.

I don't think he's touched it at all.

❖

The children I meet at the hospice are dying when I go to visit. It is called Ty Hafan – Summer House – and children die here all the time.

There is a jacuzzi and a sensory room for children who are blind and deaf, which has vibrating chairs and cushions. There are wheelchairs more like sofa beds, carers with smiles on their faces and bedrooms for parents, far enough away to sleep all night.

Joe is not dying. I just need a good night's sleep, and so does Alex, who has stayed behind at home.

Joe looks lucky to me here, amongst these children who are breaking down and dying. So full of life, so full of future. I understand here what it means to have a future.

When I get home, Alex says it's been a long weekend. He has tidied the light room and made a swing out of climbing ropes, net and karabiners, which hangs from the centre of the ceiling in the front bedroom.

We lie Joe on his tummy inside it, turning the rope, and we sit together for a while, just holding hands,
as Joe flies round the room like Peter Pan.

❖

If I hadn't been sitting in the kitchen, lifting his hand up and down, tapping it absent-mindedly on the table along to the nursery rhymes, I'd have missed this moment.

If the phone hadn't rung in the middle of his favourite tune, and I hadn't been looking in his direction when I answered it, I'd have missed the split second he raised his fist to tap without me.

It would have been just another ordinary day.

But on ordinary days, the most extraordinary things can happen. Almost by accident, in a flash, we discover a way to break through.

'Tap once for yes,' I said, lifting his hand and dropping it once on the table. 'This is twice. Tap twice for no.'

'Do you want a drink?'

No!

'A cuddle?'

No!

'More music?'

Yes!

'Do you know how much I love you, Joe?'

'Yes,' he tapped.

Today we have been talking, Joe and I.

I'm sure he understands everything I say.

I started a new section in my little gold book tonight. 'Notes on a Resurrection', I've called it, and it's already almost full with fresh ideas and games to play.

I call him by a new name in these notes.

'Joeski.'

As if he's crossed some divide in my mind,
as if he's been born again.

❖❖❖

WHEN ALEX left, the sky looked bleached out in Market Road.

He got a flat across the city, and as soon as he got there he phoned to say he wanted to come back. He said he wanted me to ask him. He said he didn't know what he wanted anymore.

He's lost more weight; he's fallen further behind on invoicing.

When Alex left, the place gaped open with emptiness. It felt like a storm had swept through a house the birds had made, and ripped it apart.

I took Joe out shopping, the day the sky was white in Market Road. I pushed him into town and wandered about for a while in the draughty arcades.

I bought a top,
had a coffee,
and, in Mothercare's changing rooms,
I curled up and wept.

❖

Waking in separate beds across the city, we think of each other, Alex and I. I can sense it and I wish he were here.

It's peaceful without him. No arguments, no sport on the radio.

I think of him late at night too, when I look round the living room.

At the flowered tablecloth slung over the hard-backed chair, at the manuals about brain damage and cerebral palsy, flanking the poetry shelves like bookends.

I think about the things he thought and saw. My hollow eyes emerging from the light-room, and the curve of my back as I cuddled Joe at night.

He comes three times or so a day to pattern and to play with Joe. The rest of the sessions I do with Judit, or with anyone else who offers – friends passing through, neighbours sometimes, parents.

But on the whole it's Alex opposite me at the table, moving arms and legs and smiling down at him.

In the mornings now, when I'm getting him dressed, we listen to Mozart, Joe and me. A site on the web says it's good for healing. After that we sit at the piano together and I name the keys. I paste orange, luminous dots all over them, but still he can't see them. I wear my sparkly wig and red lipstick in the light-room; but still he prefers to commune with the angels.

I keep my books in perfect order this winter. At the back are my lists of daily schedules and appointments, all covered still in ticks, but sometimes I imagine that I won't heal him now. That the endless stream of therapies cannot unbreak us, and that nothing whole will ever come of two such broken people.

At night I play solitaire: 'If this works out he'll talk,' I whisper to the computer; 'If this works out he'll walk... his vision will come... his hands will improve.' Sometimes the cards work out, but more often they don't. 'If this works out he'll be happy anyway,' I whisper then. 'If this works out all these games mean nothing at all.'

The health visitor says I need to look after myself more, that I look skinny, ill, and can have home help if I want it. I do. I'm getting used to them now – Kyra, small, smart and reserved, and

Jenny, tall and like a party, getting the shopping in, and tidying around me as I do Joe's therapies. They make cups of tea and will even pattern if I ask.

There are times I wonder if I'd cope without them.

Times like now, when the front door bangs and the rose petals blow up the hall, and fall like dying ballerinas all about me.

Times when the washing turns somersaults on the line, and I watch it with Joe in my arms like an anchor.

My brother says it is a sign of strength, not weakness, to accept help.

The weatherman says there's been a fall in sunlight.

❖

At the press ball, Alex says he's still in love with me.

He says it means the world to him that I've come out in my shimmering frock and big smile – old style.

He can put his troubles aside, Alex. Talk and mingle, joke and laugh with the people I once used to mingle with.

He's stayed the same and still treats me like a girl to be proud of.

We swirl round the dance-floor, round and round in each other's arms, and it feels in this moment that we are exactly who we are again.

I don't recognise myself when I go to the ladies.
The yellow, sunken cheekbone,
the face out of focus on the mirror's edge.

❖

(The Moorings)

We sing carols around the patterning table, mum and dad and I.

We take it in turns in the light room, passing Joe from knee to knee and telling him stories.

I visit the local healers.

I take him to the pantomime with Carol, Aurelia, Ambra and Teo, and William, Hari and Lilli, but it is far too much for him. His arms flail and he screams at the noise, and so we sit out in the foyer, listening to the distant echoes of boos and cheers.

When Angela, my friend from school, comes this Christmas, we lounge around my bedroom like we've always done since we've been small. She says it's the worst she's ever seen me, but that I'll come through it. She tells me she's only really loved two people in her life, that her husband is one and I am the other, so she'll make damn sure I come through it.

When Alex calls to wish me Happy New Year, we run out of things to say before the chimes have finished.

My dad says I should come home with Joe next year. He says I need to find myself again.

I walked with him today, through the empty arcades by the sea, and he talked about a book I kept when I was young. 'All the words I've ever loved,' I called it, and I kept it with me till I lost it on a bus to Whitley Bay.

He said it might help to write,
but I can't think of any words I like anymore.

My dad said I just needed to find them again.

❖

Usually he is walking towards me, taking those first, few wobbly steps, and I am clapping, spellbound.

There are always other people around, neighbours and half-forgotten school friends, who nod at me gently and say 'there you are, there you are', as if they'd known all along he would do it. Sometimes they don't notice him at all and I am waving my arms at them, wanting them to share these brief, magical moments, when dreams are so real.

Mornings are the worst of times.

I wake from these dreams to the numb sensation of Joe's curled-up body in my side, unable to move an inch until I lift him into my arms to start the day.

Alex says he dreams too now we're apart. He is always in a busy high street and Joe is walking ahead, away from him, through crowds of people. He says he sees everything at a knee-high eye level; the swinging hands and the children's faces that he totters past.

He says the light is always extraordinary when he dreams of Joe. That the hours in our light room have changed the way he thinks of light now, but in his dreams, it's always beautiful and life feels like a nightmare when he wakes.

Sometimes I think we're closer than we realise, Alex and I.

When we wake perhaps or when we're moving arms and legs.

When we're lost in the soft, dark layers as Joe sees, talks and walks through our dreams.

❖

Sian blows in with the wind one bright February morning, like a new beginning.

When I first called the agency in town to ask for a babysitter, and was told they provided 'respite workers' to mothers like me and 'care assistants' to children like Joe, I decided against it – it made me feel like I was failing him.

Now I need a break, whatever they call it.

I'm not sure what to make of Sian, this sylph-like waif with cascading chestnut hair who collapses around the place in fits of giggles and forgets her bag or coat each time she leaves.

She brings a whole new wavelength to Market Road.
She has a way about her, Sian,
she is happy.

Joe adores her. He dissolves in her arms like new love.

Perhaps people never truly know how the things they say and do affect another inside. What work they do, just by being who they are.

I don't know if Sian knows what it means to me when I see the way she talks and plays with Joe, and when the sound of their laughter reaches me as I'm lying, quietly listening, on my bed.

How her throwaway comments heal wounds I didn't know I had.

The casual way she calls him beautiful, and says she sometimes likes to pretend he's her son when she takes him out.

The way she doesn't look for milestones,

and her great love of small things.

❖

I turn left at the end of Market Road to get to Thompson Park. I
prefer it to Pontcanna Fields. It has no swings and slides and there
are better things to look at. Covert meetings between camp men,
a statue of Eros,
and a tree with an old man's face carved into its trunk.

I sit Joe in front of this tree and stand behind it, playing peep-bo
round the sides when no-one's looking. I'm still trying to get him
to look at me.

Now and again these days I think he sees my shadow. He has
started to squint at the sunshine.

❖

(Spring 2001)

It doesn't happen, the impossible, the doctors say.
But this day, after so, so many,
when we're up in the light room,
his small white fist rises in the darkness
and touches the light.

I guess we should call it a miracle – sight – in the eyes of our
once-blind child.

My mother says it feels magical,
like the seasons have found a way to answer us,
like the earth has read our buried prayers.

My father says it's amazing what hard work, love and faith can
bring.

It is amazing.

Never has the world looked more beautiful,
than it does to me this spring.

❖ ❖ ❖

THERE IS a letter from Gratia in March. I read it at the kitchen table.

It says that Ioho Blue has died. That one day last month, he just stopped breathing.

He was two years and nine months old, and was buried in his Sex Pistols t-shirt with crystals in his hands at the Valley of the Kings in La Gomera.

Gratia says she stayed up all night in the garden of remembrance, singing him songs until the daybreak.

She says it's so important to appreciate what we have, while we still have it.

❖

Easter is early, with thunderous showers. Joe likes listening to them, the sudden cracks of lightning and the scattering hail upon the windows. He likes the singing in the chapel across the road, and he likes it when Sian comes, all cold and wet and warm with happy stories.

There are new routines in Market Road. Sian helps me now. At mealtimes we push the food into the corners of his mouth to encourage him to chew, and spread Manuka honey on his lips to help him place his tongue.

At bedtime, we play his auditory integration tape, which claims to help the speech centre in the brain. This strange, foreign music lasts for ten minutes and he makes a howling sound when he listens through the earphones.

The speech therapist says this therapy is all 'pie in the sky – unproven', but I think it does something and Sian agrees. She helps with everything, Sian – the tapes, the patterning, the light room. She remembers everything I teach her – and still forgets her coat each time she leaves.

I stop going to the oxygen tanks. It doesn't feel right anymore. I don't know why. Instead, Joe has music therapy with a happy, clappy duo from the Touch Trust. They bring drums and tambourines, and he lies on the mat between them, laughing.

I still take him to the special nursery out of town, tooting my horn as we go round the windy bends of Star Lane. 'More,' I say, 'shout more and I'll toot again,' but he sits in his car-seat behind me, furiously tapping his hand on his knee.

Sue from Bristol has sent white gloves from America, which light up in the dark, and now and again I watch with awe, as his small stiff hand meets mine in the darkness.

Joanna has sent more pictures, everyday objects, in luminous reds and yellows, pinks and blues, oranges, purples, greens. Every colour of the rainbow.

We see an optometrist in Cheltenham now, a small, dark, unassuming man, who doesn't treat Joe like the woman at the eye clinic. He lies beside him on the floor in his office, studying Joe's eyes quietly while he strokes his cheek and talks to him. He says he's not so sure that Joe is blind. He says it seems to be making a difference, the work we do.

Last week the optometrist thought he saw cataracts in Joe's eyes when he looked into them from a peculiar sideways angle. He said, if he was right, something could be done to help him after all.

I made an emergency appointment to see the eye doctor I don't like at the clinic, but she said he'd given us false hope, this man. She said there were no cataracts.

When she saw us, I asked her to look into them sideways, just like the man in Cheltenham had done, but she wouldn't do it. She said she had years of medical expertise behind her opinion, and that I shouldn't waste my time and money with alternative therapists who don't.

Sian says I'll get over this. She says she knows there'll be a breakthrough for us one day.

She's strong, Sian.

I will always remember her coat in my life.

❖

Alex has bought a caravan in a remote bay in West Wales. He takes us there at weekends, all wrapped up in his silver car. He has bought a feather-soft car seat for Joe so that I can sit in the front again. We travel for miles in silence, listening to the sound of each other breathing,
and then we arrive,
to wide open sea and sky.

The place is deserted and the caravan is old and smells of plasticine but Alex has painted it bright inside. He's put black plastic bags on one bedroom window and screwed in a 240 watt bulb so that it feels like home.

We thought we'd talk when we came here, Alex and I, but usually we just sit together on the doorstep, watching the sun and the rain and the seagulls drift past.

Sometimes he carries Joe along the stony beaches on his back, and I follow behind, watching him stop here and there to dangle his feet in the sea.

In the afternoon, Alex makes sculptures out of the shells and stones I find and I make up fairytales to pass the time.

The night drifts by with Joe asleep, between us.

Alex thinks it's time to stop the routines now, the ones that 'kill us,' as he puts it. He says we've lost seasons at the patterning table and in the light room. It's time to 'choose life' again.

Alex says that when he parks his car in Market Road, he watches me sometimes before he comes in to do the patterning. He says he sees me standing in the centre of the upstairs room in tatty clothes, with my head down, turning the rope as Joe flies around me in circles.

He says I need to join the world again.

At the caravan this weekend, Alex made me a small stone sculpture which looked like a mother and child, all out of balance, with the baby too big for her arms.

Its head is made of marcasite stone, and it looks like there are stars in its skull.
'You can't hold him forever,' he said when he gave it to me.

It felt like the end of an era.

❖

Watching the litter toss itself up Market Road. Watching the sudden downpours wash the cars. Watching the mothers gather in a circle outside the chapel crèche. It's always the same at 3.15, when we go to the window, Joe and me.

And then suddenly the children will spill out, scattering the puddles and kicking their shoes, and shouting and pointing and begging for sweets, laughing with each other.

I don't think Joe sees them, but he listens quietly every day, until the roar disperses in the distance, and the rain is loud again upon the window.

Today was no different to the others, until the roar died down and I moved to carry him away.

And then slowly, stiffly and with all the will he could muster, he strained his face towards me, and rendered his very first word.

'More.'

'More,' he said.

It comes in waves – hope – like the light.

It can come with a single word when you least expect it.

❖

There is a letter from Gratia on the kitchen table. It says she's pregnant again – in less than a month!

My friends Julie and Joanna, my sister Carol, and sister-in-law Lesley, are all pregnant again too.

Suddenly, the whole world
has moved on a life.

❖❖❖

THE STEINER nursery in Pontcanna is a gentle affair. There is a regular pace to life behind the gates of the old church hall in Kings Road, and its sprawling, untamed garden.

The philosophy here is to leave undisturbed the natural rhythms of children, to allow them to dream,
to let them Be.

It feels deeper than an education.

It is what I would have wanted for him had we been normal, and it is what, after countless sleepless nights, I still want for him now.

Cath, the founder of this nursery, welcomes us with open arms. She says every child comes with a gift and that Joe's 'inner joy', is very strong.

The first day I took him he lay motionless amongst his peers, or stayed in my arms, pushing his head into my thundering heart. Cath wanted him to roll on a mat by the others, but he couldn't do it, and I couldn't bear to watch him try.

One mother said he would teach the other kids to count their blessings and I went to the toilet and cried.

It's easier now. He sits on my knee giggling at the children's words and delights in the meanings they give them. He's even started to answer them, 'yes' and 'no'.

Sometimes they call out and sometimes they forget all about him. Today a girl in a chequered pinafore came up and kissed his cheek and said: 'I love you Joe'.

He is accepted.
And to me it is enough.

At playtime he feels pine cones here, wooden toys and faceless
dolls, and during circle time I dangle him by my legs, so that he
can move round with the others at eye level.

Outside he follows them over the logs, up the trees, into the
sandpit and hedgerows, just a few steps behind in my arms.

Cath plays her flute when it's time to come in, then tells a story
and sings a song.

He's happy here.

❖

Sometimes, at the end of the day,
when sleep has composed his body
to seem almost normal in my arms,
I let the mirror swallow us whole,
assemble a balding calm over
the day's reflections,
contemplate us whole
and collect us,
picture perfect.
These days pass,
stinging tears out of glass.

❖

The oxygen tanks are closed in Swansea. The Charity
Commission is appointing a receiver as 'strong evidence
suggests' it's been mismanaged. The Commission has also

appointed a receiver and manager to The Rescue Foundation as part of a formal inquiry. People have taken its tins off their shop counters in the high street.

When I listen to the radio, I hear a doctor say that nine out of ten people who know they are going to have a disabled child choose to abort, which makes me wonder just how many more children like Joe there would be.

In the papers I read an article that says a man with cerebral palsy was attacked on the streets of Hartlepool. That Alan Powell, 32, was 'set upon' by youths and was kicked about in his wheel-chair. A neighbour, who did not wish to be named, said youths 'regularly pick on people with disabilities'.

It's a jungle out there,
and it spins such a tangled web of emotions as I stand between this world and him.
Between his profound disabilities and his tiny miracles,
between my courage and my fear,
and it makes such cobwebs of these days.

Joe says six words now: 'More, mummy, daddy, yes, no and hiya,' but the speech therapist says she cannot understand him and that he'll need a special board in time.

He has learned to recognise his colours in the light room, but the pink-lipsticked woman at the eye clinic doesn't appear to believe me.

He understands my every word, but the doctors don't seem to think so.

They don't know him like I do.

We went swimming today, to a local hotel where the water was warm. The sun was shining on the water and he laughed and squealed as I dipped him in and out, and spun him round in circles.

A smiling woman floated up to me. She said she had a friend who had a son like Joe but that she'd 'handed him over' to social services because she just couldn't cope anymore. He was at residential school now and even stayed there in the holidays.

'It's sad, isn't it?' she said, 'but they love the water, don't they?'

As she spoke to me, I tried to imagine that child for a moment, along with Joe, Jac, Marchant and Ioho Blue – all their different personalities, particular preferences and bedrooms full of fish and angels – all rolled up in one.

'No,' I answered, as she swam away, 'they don't all like the water.'

Sue says it happens all the time, this kind of thing. She said a woman stopped to talk to Marchant in the high street once and said she knew all about kids like him because she'd taught at special school.

Sue says it's as ridiculous as grouping children who wear red shoes together and that Marchant is going to go to mainstream anyway.

Such a tangled web of emotions.
Between the love and the pain,
and the light and the dark.

❖

(Lourdes, 3 years)

The 'invalid carriages' clog up the streets in Lourdes and the pavements glitter with bric-a-brac and dazzling displays of holy water.

It's hard to take seriously.
We are here for Joe's third birthday.

It's the hottest day and the air-conditioning broke in the car on the way. My sister was driving us from their hotel near Biarritz, where we're all on holiday.

We could barely breathe. We wished we'd stayed by the pool.

Joe's body feels hopeless to me this summer. Perhaps it's just the heat or the lack of things there are to do, or perhaps it's that his cousins have begun to race and leap and dive about us.

The churches don't feel any different at Lourdes. There are just more of them and still the queues for blessings are endless.

We have had Joe blessed, we have held him up to kiss the Virgin Mary, and have tried to do whatever we've been told to do.

The miracles are few and far between here, but the souvenirs and postcards are memorable. I have one with a poem about love and peace, and one with a made-up Jesus with flowers round his neck, who blows a kiss and gives a wink each time I tip it.

Driving home it feels like we've shared some crazy day trip, Carol and I. The air-conditioning begins to work again, and the car radio tunes itself mysteriously into a programme called *The Best of British Rock.*

Driving home feels almost spiritual. With the radio up sky high, and our long blonde hair and summer dresses fluttering in the wind.

❖

It's the little things that make wonder.

By the end of this summer Joe has started to open his hands more, sometimes now for more or less a minute at a time.
He's started to initiate more. Sometimes I can't get a word in.

Today he rolled over.

Sian and I were lying either side of him on the playroom floor and he worked out a way to rock his body from one side to the other, back and forth, between the two of us while we clapped and cheered with joy.

I guess it's not much for a three year old, but these little jerky rolls from side to side are quite breathtaking. They are the first of the physical milestones.

Sian says it's 'extraordinary', making new connections between his brain and his muscles, when there were none before.

Sue says Joe must be a genius. She says that for us it's the equivalent of trying to hop on one leg and wiggle the third toe along on our left foot, or something like that.

My mother says perhaps it's Lourdes that's helped him. She says maybe I should take him back again.

I don't know what to make of it.
It's wondrous I guess,
but it's still a long, long way from heaven.

❖❖❖

year four

THIS MORNING was story-book sunny and we were out in the garden, Joeski and I, smelling and touching all things green.

The leaves on the laburnum tree,
the shed,
the rosemary.

Then we lay on the swing-seat, cuddled up close under the big blue sky, reading a book called *A Fly Went By*. The saxophonist's window was closed today. The garden feels quiet when he's away.

We came in at lunchtime, and I watched the news.

People made phone calls to loved ones on the aeroplanes that hit the towers in New York.
Their last words had all been, 'I love you'.

We gave up on our therapies this afternoon, Joeski and I. We just went back to the garden and lay on the swing-seat, looking up at the sky.

'I love you,' I said.

'Blue,' he said.

I will always remember that bright blue sky.

❖

Sometimes looking through the window on these bleak autumnal days, the world looks like it's lost the will to live in Market Road.

The flights of birds from emptying trees.
The fading light,
the falling leaves.

And there are times when I wish I could join them.

Dianne Pretty wants to die. She is confined to a wheelchair and is telling the High Court that the quality of her life is so low that she wants to commit suicide.

Ramon San Pedro wanted that too when he was severely paralysed in a diving accident in Spain. He became a *cause celebre* with his Right To Die campaign.

Sometimes I wonder if this happy child,
that smiles and giggles by my side,
might also want to die one day.
Sometimes I wonder if
the time just comes
when it seems easier that way.

We've been playing cards, Joeski and me. We've made up our own special version of Old Maid which involves me showing him the cards, one by one, and then me screaming each time the Old Maid is turned.

I still believe that he might spot her first, but however many times he tries,
he still prefers his Stevie Wonder book,
with the big press buttons down the side.

Perhaps something will come to help Dianne Pretty if she just holds on,
something better than she dreams of,
something better than oblivion.

But I guess to her it doesn't seem that way.

There are thousands of women Dianne Pretty's age having face
lifts in London today, and even their toes shortened in America,
to make life feel more beautiful,
a little bit better,
a little more normal,
and they keep the doctors more than busy.

The world's a topsy-turvy place,
and despite all his best intentions,
Superman still can't
move a muscle.

Perhaps one day he will.
Perhaps Joe will remain as happy as he seems now.
Perhaps he knows it's more important to be loved, than cured.

❖

Winter is a time for letting go.

I've cut back on one patterning, and one light room session.
Judit's stopped coming.

With his enormous network of therapies Joe hasn't had much
chance to be small, much of a chance just to Be,
and so I've made a half-hearted attempt to trim them down,
and create more time for him and me.

We've been out visiting the Christmas trees across the city this
winter. We've been in the front pews of churches, singing the
carols and the back rows of theatres, shouting at the pantomimes.
We've been to all the glitzy grottos,
all the kids' shows,
I can find.

He has followed the children round the advent spiral at his
Steiner group,
with his arched feet resting on my shoes,
and he has lit his own small candle,
just the way that they do.

We've developed a new and somewhat eclectic repertoire of
games in the house this winter.

Sometimes he lies on the living room floor and I lie in the hall
and we knock the door backwards and forwards, as if we're
playing tennis, for anything up to an hour.

Sometimes we lie on the sofa, swirling batons to the trumped-up
overtures on Classic FM.

Sometimes we lie on the bed, with the bright, flashing ball on the
long piece of string, circling our heads each time he manages to
touch it.

❖

(New year 2002)

It's hard to be sure what Joe's seeing. Some filmy, diaphanous,
cobwebby blur perhaps but, whatever it is, he has started to
scream first now, when the Old Maid card's turned.

A specialist we've started to see at the university's centre of optom-
etry is quite amazed at this. She thinks he might be doing it by
colour, but there are two yellowish cards in the Old Maid pack,
and they're both edged in black.

He is starting to see the shape of things.

The New Year papers say that Martin Creed has won the Turner
Prize in London for his light bulb installation.

It's just an empty room which has a light going on and off and off and on, all day long.

The critics say it means nothing at all, his 'work of art', that it's a joke – that an electrician could have won it!

Others find it profound.

They say it makes them feel self-conscious standing there in the dark.

To me it speaks of the light inside;
the light that comes back on,
and has something to do with a miracle.

❖

I've finished my gold book now, the one with the cradle on the front, intended to record his milestones.

It suddenly seems strange looking back through these pages; all the tight, concentrated notes, scratchy drawings and massage and tapping techniques I now know by heart.

All the frantic little ticks at oxygen tanks – they add up to 96 in total.

The early notes are not like my own writing. They look styptic, nervous, as if I'm somehow afraid to slip through the gaps – intended so that someone could take over if I did.

I guess it's been a kind of odyssey, this book for me. A ritual begun in fear that has somehow come to love.

The scrawl has a lighter spirit about it towards the end; there's more space between the lines and the sentences lift at the edges.

I think this is how belief looks,
before we know what to call it.

❖❖❖

JOE IS somewhere in his fourth spring when I make a tree of blessings. I buy a lone silver birch twig that's been in the flower shop since Christmas, and write out small, white cards to hang on its branches.

Life is changing, and the saxophonist plays melodies, which float from his window to mine as I scribble in gold ink at the kitchen table.

Together, strung along the branches, these blessings are so real to me. Each impossible step turned possible.

The day 'the epilepsy' disappeared and he began to smile again.
The day he rolled over,
and the day he squinted at the sunshine after the countless days when he did not.
The day he saw Old Maid.
The day he hugged me.

Joe's blessings have been full of crossings over,
blind to seeing,
silent to speaking,
and from a place where he couldn't communicate his wants or fears, to a life where he now can.

My tree gives me another sense of reality.

It pleases me to decorate its branches,
and pass it on the dresser in the kitchen,
all dressed up with snow-white cards.

❖

His walking frame is red and made of iron, with belts and buckles at the chest and hip, and two ready-made shoes that dangle at the end of two jointed bars of steel, skilfully prompting his step.

It fits him fine.

We took it to Steiner today and I nudged him forwards down the incline towards the children.

He looked like a renaissance prince tip-toeing amongst them under the trees,
like the uncommon butterfly,
released.

I wrote out another card tonight.

'Joe walked,' it said.

I've hung it on my tree of blessings,
so that it's there to meet me,
when I come down the stairs tomorrow morning.

❖ ❖ ❖

THE CATARACTS are diagnosed in May. I watch the pink lips of the eye doctor tell me what I told her a year ago. I wait for her apology but it does not come. She says Joe has been a difficult child to assess, and that it was difficult to get a good look at him.

The cataracts are dense now apparently and right over the centre of both eyes. After three years of telling us he's blind, she just says she 'seems to have been mistaken'.

The optometrist in Cheltenham, whose letter she dismissed, says we've lost critical time.

We have been assigned a new eye doctor at the clinic now who is kind and courteous. He thinks Joe's visual problems are much more likely to do with the messages in the brain than the eye itself, so it's unlikely it will really make much difference.
'But still,' he says, 'no doubt,
it's better that they're out!'

The new doctor has scheduled the operation as an emergency, and his predecessor has completely disappeared from view.

❖

It feels like forever, when they take him up to theatre, but it's just an hour on the clock on the ward. I know there can't be a miracle when he opens his eyes, but it's one less barrier, one less thing to fight against.

There is another boy in our corner of ward eleven, in the next bed to ours. His name is David and he's almost three. David stares at the ceiling, arching backwards all the time and has had a tube put in his stomach to help him feed.

His foster mother, Jane, sits calmly by his bedside in a neat suit, and wears a neat grey bob around her face. When David cries and shudders, she rearranges him gently, one way, then the other, and kisses his forehead. He's totally blind, has severe cerebral palsy, severe epilepsy and won't get any better, Jane tells me. She says his mother couldn't cope, and that she has fostered kids like him for years.

We've talked a lot, Jane and I, in this corner on ward eleven. Early this morning, when Joe was walking round in the frame that prompts his step, shouting 'hiya' at the nurses and bumping into everything, she said he showed such a love of life that it was hard to imagine he'd once been like David.

She made notes about the fish oils and the treatments I give him, and said she'd discuss it with his mother.

His mother came in this afternoon. She was here for the very same hour that Joe was up in theatre and she sat on David's bed, kicking her legs in jeans and trainers.

She picked him up for a moment before she left, buried her face in his neck and clasped him tightly to her chest, before she put him down again.

Jane says his mother loves him so much, she simply cannot bear it.

Mothers who leave and mothers who don't,
we're all the same.

❖

Joe has glasses. Big, round, national health, plastic glasses. I am so proud of them.

We had our picture taken in the photograph booth in Woollies this week. He sat on my knee, laughing his head off, shouting 'more, more, again peas,' when the light flashed on. And I was laughing too.

This is my favourite picture.

Shaggy blond hair, cheeky smile, rosy cheeks, head only slightly tilted on my shoulder and my shoulder only slightly forward to support it. Glasses, big, round and shiny, just like Harry Potter.

I love it with all my heart.

Our new eye doctor phoned today to say the second cataract can come out soon, and that he'll also try to correct Joe's squint next year.

It's funny now I look at this picture.
The squint's really quite bad I suppose,
and yet I hardly even notice it now.

❖

When Gratia comes to Market Road she brings Iona. Her brand new baby girl, textbook in every way.

She says life is totally different with Iona, that there's no comparison to last time round.

We hang out just like we used to, Gratia and I. About the house or around the therapy rooms of Joe's appointments, but I already see the different world she lives in.

I can see how easy and how safe it is when therapy's not needed. I can sense how it feels, when people stop to admire her baby on the street.

I see Joanna with Callum and Jude these days, and Julie with Freya and Clara. Sometimes Julie sends Joe tapes of Freya telling stories with Clara gurgling in the background.

I know how nice life can be with perfect babies.

I guess I just notice it more, when I'm with Gratia.

❖

We go out more now, Joeski and me. We make special outings with the built-up walker, and the built-up bike that I pull along behind me on a pole.

The staring seems less these days, but maybe I've just got used to it.

It matters less perhaps – it's normal.

I take him to the supermarket, where we play in the aisles of light and space and mirrors, and he learns to tell my face from the crowd. We spend time with the fruit and veg, and get lost in the aromas of pineapples, as the world rushes past us filling its trolleys.

We go to the red brick art centre on the corner of Market Road to see the exhibitions.

And we go to the park,
both parks,
again.

Sometimes he likes to touch the trees or smell the flowers when we're walking side by side each other at snail's pace.

Sometimes he likes to hang around outside the playground, where the other kids gather and life's all swings and roundabouts.

I am beyond the staring now. I've lost my fear of it and have found a new sense of calm in our small private rituals in the wide-open spaces of this city.

Today, when we reached the playground I took him inside and he sat on my knee on the swing and the roundabout, then climbed in my arms up the slide.

I was out of breath when I got him to the top, and when I looked down I saw a sea of upturned heads, all looking back towards our piece of sky.

Today I discovered that fear
comes second
to love.

❖

(Malagny
Summer 2002)

My sister has set the table in the orchard, and tied balloons to the trees. The air smells of roses and the sun lies in streaks across the table.

The damsons can hardly bear their own weight and fall here and there, at intervals, with a thud on the dry ground.

His fourth birthday is the stillest of days.

Malagny is taking its siesta; Carol and her baby Louis, Aurelia, Ambra, Teo and Joe, all daydreaming inside the blue and white farmhouse.

It's been magical here this summer. Early in the morning, we hear the song of the tiny, brown chaffinch who comes to sit at our windowsill, and then comes the roar of his cousins who fly through the door and bounce about us on the bed.

They've got closer to him now. I can see it in the way they are with him, and the things they tell him when they're walking by his side. I see it in the way they battle to understand what he battles to tell them. I see it in the way they make each other laugh.

Ambra says, 'he's a real boy now, a real boy,' and tells us that on the trampoline, he's been telling her: 'I wan a e ka-ga-oo,' when he wants her to jump with him like a kangaroo.

Carol says Joe's a different child altogether to the boy we took to Chavenoz. She takes him off to Shoppee in her soft-top yellow sports car, and buys him expensive French treats.

He sits in the back and holds his arms out like they're wings, snow-white hair like feathers in the wind.

The village is stirring now and the church clock is chiming two across the colza fields. I can hear the occasional rumble of a distant car as I pass through the splintered light and shadow of the trees.

Ambling up to the birthday table, a discarded doll gets caught under my flip-flop.

'Let's take a walk,' it squawks and totters off across the grass.

The table-cloth ripples lethargically and a damson drops dead in its centre.

They'll be awake soon, I guess.

I should go in now and dress him for his party.

He will be lying as I left him on the bed, arms outstretched, nappy loose like a tiny Christ, piercings of light from the

weather-beaten shutters,
like goldust on his body.

How exquisite it would be if today could bring a miracle.

If only he could wake to feel his body,
and come running out into this orchard
to sing and dance
amongst the children at his table.

❖

It ends well, summer. We've all made breakthroughs, in our own small ways.

Alex runs the Cardiff marathon and has his picture in the paper. He has a medal round his neck, and Joe in his arms, and they both wear the smiles of champions.

Sian passes her exams and falls in love with a footballer from Pontypridd.

And Joe makes steady progress. Everyone thinks so in Market Road – Kyra and Jenny with their smiles and their shopping, The duo with their drums and tambourines, the massage lady, the speech therapist, even the physio says he's doing well.

We are doing a new therapy now. Joe sits in a chair from Oswestry, belted up to the chest, and we rock him backwards and forwards while he leans from side to side to touch the toys that we hold out for him. Every day we hold them just a little higher, just a little bit wider and just a little bit further away.

We put the belt down a notch if he gets there, working the muscles in his torso band by band. Alex thinks he's getting stronger; and turns up every day to do it. He thinks Joe could possibly be strong enough to sit up alone quite soon, and says his speech is getting clearer all the time.

I heard Joe tell Alex he loved him today, and Alex answer that he loved him too without having to check what he'd said at all.

We've all made breakthroughs.

New toys have brought new blessings to Market Road this summer. Joe drives an electric orange car now with a joystick, and spins round in circles in the car park.

He has a brand new, sky-blue, walking frame, without belts and buckles and irons to prompt his feet, and hangs inside it, inching along on his toes.

These are his first real steps I suppose.

The old man from Preswylfa Street, who passes this way, stopped to talk for a while when we were practising today.

'There you are,' he said with a smile.
'He's mobile at last.
There you are, there you are.'

It felt like a dream.

He asked me if I'd noticed the rosebuds when he left.

I think he was trying to tell me something, the old man from Preswylfa Street, when he passed this way today.

To slow down maybe and take a little time just to enjoy these steps for what they are.

Not miracles perhaps, not all I dreamed of, but Joe's own small steps nonetheless.

When we started back across the road, I noticed the roses. They're earlier this year.

year five

IT WAS the wheelchair first.

Black and built up with headrest, footplates, shoulder straps, a pommel to keep his legs apart, a harness to secure him, and twice the size he really needed.

The man at the clinic said it 'allowed room to grow into'. It'd 'still fit,' he said, in three year's time, and we had to be 'realistic'. Joe struggled as he strapped him in, his angelic face turned towards me, straining to get his words out.

'I want to walk mummy,' he said.

Everyone was encouraging when I brought it home. Christine next door said it really wasn't so bad; that there were loads around just like it and Ray said it was nice, in fact, to see Joe sat so straight, which was by far the most important thing. Dad offered to buy a new one on the phone, specially made, he said, just as I'd like it. Alex said he'd tart it up a bit with some of those psychedelic wheel discs and luminous paints.

It wasn't the end of the world, everyone said that; but it seemed to cast a shadow, hanging about the place, next to his racy orange car and sky-blue walking frame, stealing the limelight from his Peter Pan swing and his old special chair now recovered in flowers.

It was like the arch-enemy had come home.

We've hardly used it this autumn, Joe and I. 'I want to walk,' he says, a hundred times a day, and so we go out in the walking frame all the time, while it sits in the dark under the stairs.

We go to the exhibitions at Chapter, where the floors are smooth and shiny and we go to the library round the corner, where the librarian saves him stories with clear, bright pictures. 'Tankoo Liz,' he shouts when he walks out again, and she puts her finger to her mouth and waves at him, as everyone returns to their books again. He's happiest when he's walking, Joeski – he holds his head up better, as if he's proud of himself.

I don't take the wheelchair to Steiner either.

It's moved across town, to pale pink rooms at the top of a narrow staircase in Splott. I couldn't get it up them, not even if I tried.

His pale pink days feel numbered now the days are getting darker. For all his progress, the Steiner kids have grown up around him, and for all my longing, when the other mothers talk about primary schools, we don't fit in.

The letter on the kitchen table says it isn't up to me where Joe can go to school. He must be assessed, approved and statemented, it says, and it is something that will be decided by experts.

The roses are whiter than his hair this autumn.

Just by a shade or two,

now his baby years are over.

❖

The experts don't see Joe like I do.

I can tell by the way they try to fit him into boxes, and the way they try to write him up in black and white. I can tell by the way

that they smile, with their heads tilted sideways.
And the way,
they don't appear to listen
to a word I say.

The experts say Joe has such multi-complex needs, and they use
such multi-complex phrases to define him, it's hard sometimes
to know what they see, but it's not what I see.

I talk about his progress when they come,
the way he's achieved so many impossibles,
how he's learned to see, and learned to talk,
learned to roll and, in whatever fashion, has learned to walk.
I tell them he's come so far
he's something of a superstar,
I tell them he gets every word we say,
that I think he's quite bright,
and needs a tailored education.

They visit us time and again, the experts. They tick a few more
boxes and ask me lots of things that I don't know,
and I get this feeling when they come and go, that they really
don't see him like I do.

It's started to feel so very small
to be me –
'mum' –
the one who knows him best of all.

❖

(Daybreak)

They're such black letter days, this autumn.
They begin with the thud of the heaviest reports, and I'm up half
of the night reading them.

All those multi-complex phrases that define us,
all those multi-complex issues,
all so neatly typed
in black and white.

Between these bold black words
and this cold white matter,
I've almost lost sight
of the boy I used to know.

The psychologist's report came yesterday. It was the very last one to come and I've read it over and over all night long.

I can still remember him here, the psychologist, with his EP charts, his questions and his Parker pen. I used it to write Joe's words on a piece of paper at first, so that he could tune his ear into the garbled sound, and then the two of them went on by themselves.

I can still remember the poem Joe told him too. 'I am a bird, I fly high, up and away in the sky,' he said, as the psychologist nodded and smiled, his head tipped sideways, packing up his pen and his charts into his briefcase.

The psychologist hasn't used big words at all in his report.

He's just put that Joe's intellect is in the average range.

'Average' – normal.

And it seems such a simple, insignificant word, amidst all his vast complexities,
that it's strange to think that's it's the one
that proves so many other experts wrong.

He has normal intelligence now,
this boy that 'wouldn't even know us!'

I've been up on the window seat all night long, going over the psychologist's report.

The street has been empty, thick with fog, and now the chapel windows have turned glassy grey with sky.

Last night I learned that
nothing's black and white,
that kids can't really be defined,
and I've learned to take,
one daybreak,
at a time.

❖

It seems simple on the face of it. There are only two suitable schools.

One is Craig-y-Parc, the other is the local special needs. They're both in Cardiff and it's quite clear cut to me which he should go to.
He's been visiting the Craig-y-Parc nursery since he was small.
He knows them there and they know him.
He's happy.
He's used to the conductive therapy they do,
he's making progress.
It's a 'specialist centre' for children with cerebral palsy,
the classes are small,
and they let the children like him use walkers!

The local special needs school does not encourage kids with Joe's level of cerebral palsy to walk. The physiotherapist says it can increase stiffness, that they do better using wheelchairs. There are children with autism, behavioural difficulties, spina-bifida and various other special needs to see to too.
The therapies are few and far between,
it's almost bursting at the seams.

The Authority says it is not up to me where Joe will go. It says he's been assessed, approved, and the experts agree that he'd fit into this school quite nicely.

The Authority has made its decision.
It doesn't answer my letters or phone calls now.
It says it's final,
and if I don't like that,
I can take it to tribunal.

I don't – so I do.

❖

It's hard to consider what is 'necessary and adequate' for any human being.
Especially my child.

His is the life that sustains me,
the blood that stops me growing old,
his is the hand that when I die,
I'll want to hold.

He'll always deserve better.

It's taken all winter to learn the complexities about the tribunal. What his needs mean in the legal jargon that defines them. What is strictly 'adequate and necessary,' to meet them.

Craig-y-Parc conductive school is private, costly and not necessary, the Authority says. So it's a battle of wills at the end of the day.

We have a polarised take on everything, the Authority and I.

Different schools of thought,

different costs to bear,
different needs to consider.

We're as far apart
as lions are to lambs
at heart.

❖

(At the Planetarium,
Baker St, London)

Julie says it calms her, looking up into space through this velvet,
rounded sky.

The man at the Planetarium says no-one really comprehends it,
though people seem to think it puts things in perspective.

It's just an average-sized yellow star, on one of the spiral-armed
edges of our galaxy, the sun.
Though it's as central to its universe,
as this fair-haired child is to mine.

Everything's relative,
Joeski appreciating the stars, and Freya now with questions on
infinity, that none of us can answer.

It's been a droplet in the sea of time; this winter turned spring,
yet it's seemed like an eternity to me.

The conductive school up Star Lane is just a stone's throw from
our house in Market Road, and yet it's seemed a million miles
away, perpetually out of orbit.

The tribunal was seven hours long,
and the panel is still debating
all the pros and cons.

I guess his future's in the stars,
between evens and odds,
in the lap of the gods,
while we kill time in dark places,
gazing up at all these heavenly bodies,
worlds away,
in quiet contemplation.

❖

It arrived at the end of a week of goodbyes, the letter from the tribunal.

Sian left for London on Monday, for a brand new life with her footballer from Pontypridd. She promised to keep in touch, and took her coat.

Joeski left Steiner on the Tuesday. The kids held his hand at circle time, pulled him round a few times in a cardboard box attached to a piece of rope, and painted him sunsets and rainbows.

And it was the week I turned forty.

The house was like a funeral parlour. Everyone sent flowers and I wandered around amongst them feeling wilted and tired, like something past its sell-by-date, something now reduced.

It was the week Joe first felt heavy,
the week a girl in the park happened to mention in passing that she'd seen Alex out with someone else.

It seemed to arrive at the end of everything, Joe's statement.

And although it was everything I wanted,
and had every single thing I'd fought for,

typed up crisp and clear
in black and white,

it still took a while to sink in
that I'd won.

❖❖❖

I'M FINE taking him.

In the car up Star Lane, tooting my horn, around the windy bends and him shouting, 'More, mummy do it again'. I think of the times I prayed for this.

We are laughing. The sun is shining.

I'm fine going in.

Up through the corridors of wheelchairs to the light at the end of the hall and the brightly coloured rooms of the conductive centre. It is next to the swimming pool, which has hot blue water to relax his muscles and there are smiling conductors milling around and walking frames round the doors.

'I want to walk,' he says as we pass them, and it is enough to know that here, for now at least, he'll be allowed to walk to his heart's content.

The headmaster meets us and shakes his hand. 'Hello Joeski,' he says warmly, and Joe answers him back, all cock-a-hoop, then joins the others. There are five kids in his class and, at the table, there are five special chairs shaped like tigers and giraffes. The teacher, who knows him from nursery, seats him by the window, which has a view of the cherry blossom trees.

His little, blond head has dropped on his shoulder at a right angle to that window when I leave, and walking back past the long lines of wheelchairs, I now see how they increase in size to adult years. I can hear him calling out to me when I reach the foyer, shouting words that I'm quite sure no-one else will understand.

The light's so sharp,
so empty with freedom when I reach the door,

that my arms and legs move into it,
as if they've left their soul behind.

This physical separation has a unique numbness to it.
We can't complete each other anymore.

I break my heart going home.
There is a monsoon inside me.

❖

The days begin around seven now. He will wake and call for his music, and I'll get up and find nursery rhymes or Mozart, whichever he asks for.

I'll massage his hands and feet with sage cream, and then I'll roll him over into my arms to wash and dress him in his red and yellow uniform. He will ask for porridge and toast and sit at the breakfast table on my knee, resting his head on my shoulder and telling me he does not want to go to school.

Before the special taxi comes, I brush his tangled hair and write notes to his teachers in his exercise book. I think of the things he may want to tell them, the things he may ask for that they might not understand, and then I write out how these words sound, every one of them.

He brings me notes back at the end of the day, short and sweet one-liners: 'He's settling in fine,' they say.

He is so vulnerable; I cannot bear it.

Every time he goes,
I sit amongst the breakfast pots and pans,
and cannot bear it.

The man on the radio plays melodies to mothers on the school run. One for Sam, who has three under eight, running her off her feet. One for Jackie whose four year old plays the piano. This one for Rachel and the 'two little terrors that drive her mad'. They all sound the same to me,
blessed,
and I want it for him
and I want it for me,
so badly.

I can't stand the fact that I can't heal him. Can't stand the fact I can't protect him from all those corridors of wheelchairs, can't give him all those stolen landscapes and long-lost freedoms.

I can't bear his heartbreak when it comes...

It's bound to come.

Sometimes, when the taxi's gone, I go back to bed or lie on the sofa in my nightie watching the blonde presenter I once shared a desk with, reading breakfast news.

She wears a tailored suit now and patent shoes.
We're satellites apart.

Sometimes I think of the girl I saw up at Joe's school. I can't stop thinking of her. She was in the corridor one day in a summer dress, pale pink cardigan and black metal wheelchair which had a fluffy headrest and perspex tray. She held her hand awkwardly and leaned backwards, straining her neck to say something, just like Joe does, but I couldn't understand her. The IT teacher told me she'd be eighteen soon. She said she was bright, this girl, quite similar to Joe.

Sometimes, these days, I don't move from the kitchen table. I just sit here alone, talking to God.

I don't ask for miracles now. 'Just a sign,' I say, to tell me what it is that I'm supposed to do.

Just one small sign,
to pull me through.

❖

The first day I went out, I took the bus to town.

There was a health show at the university and I walked up and down the aisles, up and down the cure-alls and remedies, looking for something new, something I hadn't yet tried.

But there was nothing I hadn't tried.

I went to a lecture called: 'Healing the body and healing the mind,' by a man who had scruffy dark hair, a hole in his jumper and was really quite funny at times.

I talked to him after, when he'd packed up his notes and was walking back to the coffee bar, and he gave me his card which said: 'We can all heal our heartbreaks – whatever they are'.

For a moment I felt he'd read my mind.

For a moment it seemed like God had sent him.

❖

I see him on Thursday afternoons, David, the guy from the health show. He works from home, not far from me, on the same side of the city.

I should walk, but I take the car and I drive the way I go to Joe's school, turning right at the lights half way,
into a landscape between things,
with sycamore trees and small, white, suburban houses with a garage on the side.

The first time I came, he hugged me on the doorstep and took me inside to a room at the back with some bookshelves and a view of the garden. I sat there while he made some tea, watching a small white dog running around the blue and pink azaleas.

When he came back in and asked me how I was, I said I had no idea and started to cry.

It seemed such a silly thing to cry about at the time, but I've cried with him for weeks now in this small back room, on warm suburban afternoons.

The counsellor calls it a journey, the time we spend together here.

'Like a road trip,' he says, round the rough map of my heart.

I guess it adds some drama, passing towns called Guilt and cities called Grief,
amongst the pink and blue azaleas.

❖❖❖

AMY WAS born in June. Joanna said she felt like 'the cat who'd got the cream'. A pretty little sister for Callum and Jude – she'd had everything she wanted.

Life was perfect for Joanna.
She had a sense of the goddess about her.

Amy was still brand new when she brought her, already lifting her arms and grasping a rattle. She made eye contact, blew bubbles, and held her head up strong.

We made a pact once, Joanna and I. We said we'd never compare our children and we'd never hide our feelings from each other, but I sometimes hide them now she comes with Amy.

It's a mixed up midsummer 2003.

I tell people I'm getting over things; but I'm not. I say I'm better than I was, more contented, especially since the tribunal, but I'm not, not really.

Between the grief and the longing, there are cul-de-sacs of pain.

I hit them in the morning, before I get him off to school. When I wash and squash and squeeze him into his brand new, multi-zipped Lycra undersuit from his ankles to his neck which, for £400, promises more proprioceptive feedback between muscles and brain. It is suitably named 'a second skin'. He tries to stop me sometimes and I run the zips up faster so they sound like a train, which always makes him laugh again.

Then I fix the two hard plastic splints to his feet, fastening them up to the knee to straighten him out, and lift him into his wheel-chair to start his day. I belt him neatly at the hips and shoulders to stop him falling sideways and strap his feet firmly onto the footplates, so that he won't slide down. To finish, I put a patch over his right eye to strengthen the vision in the left, which I think is weaker, but I could be wrong – no-one's really confirmed it – and then, matter of fact, put his glasses on.

Sometimes now he'll lift his hand to knock them off again, teasing me, and I, secretly delighted by his achievement, feign crossness and insist he puts them on again.

These are the games that we play.

There are cul-de-sacs at night too.

When I put him to bed and kiss him goodnight, and insist I'll be cross if he does not go to sleep.

I'm writing my lists at the kitchen table, and it starts like this:
'Mummy, I can't go to sleep.'
'Go to sleep now Joe, or I'll be cross.'
'May I have another story?'
'No!'
'A glass of water?'
'No!'
'Mummy – I'm falling.'

I run back upstairs now and catch him just in time, just in time before he falls. I suppose I realise the will it's taken him to do it. All those impossible thought patterns he's mastered and the mighty effort it's taken him to move his body so that he's falling and I'll come running back again. The longing must be desperate that precedes it. 'Tankoo,' he says as I hold him in the dark, gently rocking, re-conjoined.

These days it seems everything's black that comes out of the blue.

The OT says I must start to think about stairlifts, bathroom aids and hoists. 'A disabled child disables a family,' she says, over her cup of tea, one day. Despite my protests, the speech therapist puts his name down on the list for a communication aid and still doesn't believe he'll speak 'effectively', so that other people 'really understand him properly'.

People say it's time to start my life again now Joe's going off to school. They say that my life is different from his,
and that it's time to move on.

But they don't know how it is for me.

My whole world has cerebral palsy,
whether I'm with Joe,
or not.

❖

'He's nearly five.' Alex says it, every time he leaves. He thinks we've chased enough miracles and tried enough things.

He mentions things we haven't thought of, things we haven't spoken of for years. Things the doctors used to say.

Alex says we'll burn ourselves out, all the therapies we're doing. That there are parents like us, not five but eighteen years later, and still nothing's really changed.

Parents who've gone to America, parents who've gone mad, parents who've moved heaven and earth, and are still wheeling their child into exactly the same places. Alex doesn't believe our 'time-consuming therapies' can change much anymore. 'There's no proof,' he says, just like a doctor now.

'But he's not even five,' I say back to him, and then we just stand together, out on the doorstep, looking back and forth at one another, both trying to figure out why time should have something to do with it.

Alex bought his first single when he was five. I moved to The Moorings and put my dolls around the fireplace in my room. We can still remember the things we did, the things we imagined, the things we understood and knew.

We'd hoped for more for Joe at five;
and now five looms before us,
like the end of the world.

I still go back to the doctors, just to check if there is anything, 'anything at all'. I go back to the therapists – even the ones I once gave up on, and back to the healers, just in case.

One bright June morning I take him on the train to see Uri Geller. My friend Penny picks us up at the station in Reading and drives us through his wrought-iron gates and we all have tea in his room full of crystals.

'Tell me what he sees,' I asked him. 'Like you do on the telly.' But he couldn't do it, not for Joe.

He gave us a signed bent spoon when we left.

I laugh about it with David one wet, black afternoon as his small white dog runs round the pink and blue azaleas.

'I'll never give up,' I tell him.

'I can't give up until I've healed him.'

David says I've reached a place called Sacrifice.

❖

The papers are full to bursting with five-year-old champions. Egg and spoon races, cartwheels, hops and skips and jumps. I look at them before I go to his sports day.

I sit with a select group of mothers and watch the conductor help him splash his arms about in the swimming pool, watch him struggle to hold a ball and watch him roll himself over towards the edge of a blue shiny mat.

'I did it, mummy,' he shouts out as his teacher pins a red rosette upon his jumper, and hangs a medal round his neck for 'trying hard'.

I clap and cheer as if he's crossed the Amazon.

I try so hard at being happy,
but every battle he wins these days feels hollow.

❖

I spend all summer in Sacrifice.

Fighting passing thoughts and passing feelings.

I fight the ones that make me cry at night and those that come when I'm alone.
I fight the ones that drop in unexpectedly and the ones that make themselves at home.

Everything's a battle on the inside.

There are the letters I write to charities,
the new equipment I can't lift upstairs
the strangers, who ask God to bless him,
or give him money at the summer fairs.
There are the boys in the park who throw stones at the ducks
and follow us with their eyes.
There are countless fears
that flutter up inside.

And steps,
everywhere –
thousands of them!

There are so many places where I make a fuss,
because his wants or needs
are not considered as important as
the rest of us,
my heart's become a warrior's shield,
and the city,
like a battlefield.

We escaped to The Moorings this summer, Joeski and I, but no
matter how many picnics and stories and songs we had, no
matter how many times mum sunbathed beside us, dad mowed
the lawns and the sun passed over, turning the windows into
glitter, it wasn't like it used to be. The Moorings was up for sale,
the sun felt cold and my parents talked a lot of getting old.

Summer has quite forgotten itself this year,
and has so little to say,
that when our blue badge came the other day
we went out to celebrate, Joeski and me,
and parked all over the city,
on double-yellow lines.

❖

(five years)

I put hyacinths on the table and Alex arrives with a car-full of
blown-up balloons.

Marchant comes from Bristol, Julie and Freya from London,
everyone from the Steiner school.

It's the party of parties, the best in town; we have cake, games and music and Paddy the Clown.

Later, when they've all gone home, we have a barbecue, Alex and I.

We get drunker, turn up the stereo even louder, and dance together under the stars, twirling our laughing child, one then the other, around the flames.

It's early morning, when they're both asleep,
and there's no-one about but the moon,
that I sob my heart out.

Still the same old grief,
still the same old longing.

❖

David calls it progress, this secret sobbing I do.

He says it's the only way out,
the only way on,
the only way through.

He says there's no overnight sleeper out of Sacrifice.

year six

'TA RA luv,' he shouts out, when the taxi comes, and sets off with his elderly escorts, the three of them collapsing in giggles. 'We taught him that,' they shout back to me excitedly. 'He's real Cardiff now.'

I stand on the doorstep this autumn, waving at their three white heads which bob about as the taxi pulls away. He is singing a song and they are singing with him. He doesn't look back – not once.

'He's made mates,' I think, as he disappears up Market Road to his world away from me. He sings all the way, they tell me. That's how they've learned to understand his words, they say. That's how he teaches them.

Joe is, school says, a spirited child and has settled in well this term. He does not ask for me. He likes to laugh, they say, and enjoys the music, especially the singing in assembly, and the disco every Friday where he sits in his wheelchair and kicks his legs in time with Scott and Kylie.

The teachers have rigged up a switch for him, and say that now he presses a button to answer questions of multiple choice it takes half the time it does to get his words out, and they are quite amazed by what he knows and understands. They have started to think he might be 'bright'. Bright, this child that wouldn't know us – next year perhaps, he'll be a genius!

His message book has gold and silver stars – 'Good Days' – his teachers call them, and his life without me appears to be full of them.

Yesterday is gone. Dried up and dropping with the leaves.
The birds have flown and the shifting skies look big and
strangely bare.
He has moved on, and does not need me there.

And, now he sings in other worlds,
and has suddenly let me go,
it's this I know.
That love grows even stronger in the wide, empty spaces of his
absence
and next to this all problems evaporate like dreams.
It's him I'm missing now,
not what might have been.

                                    ❖

The pictures on the dresser in the kitchen span five years now.
Alex on assignment in his black polo-neck and raincoat at the
Eiffel Tower, the most handsome man in the world, and one with
me and my big, round tummy, watching the dolphins swim in
Cardigan Bay. Joe in a baggy blue suit leaving hospital, and one
with my mother by the rose tree.

Joanna, Julie and I with our bellies then our babies, arms around
each other, smiling. Callum and Freya up on the cliffs in shorts
and stripy t-shirts like *Swallows and Amazons*, Ambra in a field
of golden corn, Joe in a poppy field, and the photo booth at
Woolworths,
on a swing,
on a bed, on a knee
laughing next to a Christmas tree,
family all about him.

These are my chosen pictures, the ones I display, and the ones
that in their own perfectly-poised and soft focus way have
sustained me, smiling back each day. You can't tell from these

photos that there's anything wrong, anything different, they look quite normal.

Alex has given me pictures too, today, a dozen or so of his 'journeys with Joe', as he calls them.

There are a few of their weekend trips up the valleys together, sitting on mountains or waiting for trains – Bridgend, Cwmbran, Pontlottyn, where he said they got off, smiled, and got back on again.

And there are a few a little closer to home. These he's shot in black and white, neatly captioned, and are now laid out across my kitchen table.

The one of Joe in the throngs of the crowd at the football match on City Road, a blaze of the bluebirds all about him, has been captioned: *one in a million*.

The one of Joe at school, wearing a corset, splints, and a patch on his eye, and the one at the Rubicon dance centre, kicking his legs in his shiny black wheelchair as the ballerinas skip and twirl and fly around him. Both have *Spirit* written on the back.

I've lost hours today, glancing back and forth between the dresser and the kitchen table, looking at these black and whites the way you do those 3D pictures that need time and effort to really see their meaning.

Minutes before Joe came back home,
I took the old ones down,
and put the new ones in their place.

❖

I carry Joe on my back now to the places we can't get to any other way. Up and along the beaches at Southerndown, up to the tops of double-decker buses and up to the 1,000 acres of rural artspace outside Cowbridge that's known as Coed Hills.

The Steiner club meets here on Saturdays, and he drifts above the tangled sprawl of children, suspended in my back-pack, adding the happiest broken note to their choir.

Winter is upon us now.

Amongst these moonspun mushrooms and dream-caught birds, he is growing too heavy to carry,

the magic's running out,

and the trees look like upside-down broomsticks at this time of year.

❖

On the stage, it's hard to spot him. With his sky-blue frame and lopsided pose, he looks just like the rest here. An orphan in *Oliver Twist*, and there are lots of orphans, lots of frames and lots of kids inside them in rags and caps, with soot on their cheeks and smiles on their faces.

The conductors are like shepherds behind them, correcting a twisted limb here, a fallen head there, wiping sweet little mouths everywhere. And behind them are the wheelchairs, some almost dainty, some industrially wide, and one like a hospital bed, with cushions and a horizontal, curly-haired child inside.

Oliver Twist is a boy on crutches who speaks through a synthesiser. 'Please sir,' he says, when he presses the yellow button, 'May I have more?'

The artful dodger is a teacher, and the dance, choreographed beautifully by teenage girls in electric wheelchairs holding baskets of flowers, brings one group of parents to their feet.

The chorus, full of determined strikes of the piano, abandoned shouts, uninterpretable wailings and extra-loud conductors, is like nothing I've ever heard before.

This end of term at Craig-y-Parc school has a paralysing effect on me.
I can't move a muscle,
until Alex appears and takes my hand,
and suddenly I hear the singing,
feel my body,
and see Spirit staged before me,
in all its glory.

❖

My sister is at pains this year to point things out to me.

She thinks it's time to change my life now, go back to work perhaps, get a hobby, be something more like the 'feisty' girl I was before.

My sister says that if I keep my life on hold, before I know it I'll be old.

Joe's become one of the crowd in Malagny this Christmas and can be much more a part of things. If the girls watch videos so can he,
and if the boys play guitars he can too now,
one that has buttons in the place of strings.

He has started to sleep when everyone sleeps, eat what every-one eats and I write him a part in our Christmas play. This year

we staged it on the sofa and Joe was the spaceman who we
pretended had crashed there with fistfuls of secrets and stardust,
just like *The Little Prince*.

Sometimes I think Joe's life is now as full as any other,
perhaps sometimes even better,
I didn't do the half of what he does at his age
with the passion he enjoys it.
I didn't love to sing and dance,
had never heard of Beethoven,
and I didn't have a fraction of
his quite amazing spirit.

I'm also aware Joe's life would be fine
if I began to lead a little more of mine,
it's just my heart that doesn't seem to get it.

Every hour that I'm awake I want to heal him,
every night when I go to bed,
when we can't get his wheelchair close to the holly,
when the candles burn my eyes at church in Virry
and I ask the priest to pour more water on his head.

We walked and pushed the kids round Lake Geneva, the night
before I left Malagny. My sister pointed out Rousseau's island
and the sparkling jet d'eau.

It was the start of a brand new year and the trees looked beautiful.
Huge, white lights hanging in their branches,
like suspended moons
splayed out across an inky sky.

Joe could see them.

My heart's an ocean of storms this Christmas,
every minute
I want to heal him.

❖

It is a kind of limbo, New Year,
time is lost, time is not yet.
Full of hazard lights and thick grey fog,
and people looking inwards,
while they're out there, seeking God.

There are courses galore in Cardiff, and a thousand pieces in *The Guardian* about the thousand paths,
the thousand books,
and the thousand ways to change your life.
There's doctors' advice, tips from the stars
and all the new age stuff
which claims people who aren't happy,
just don't love themselves enough.

My mother's joining a golf club this year. It helps her not to think of things, she says. Alex is doing Buddhist meditation, Sian stage three Tai Kwon Do, and Sue's doing an Alpha Course in Bristol. Sue says when Marchant was in a coma, God spoke to him and told him 'I bring you this body to bring love', and that it's given her a whole new direction.

Gratia plans to go to La Gomera in the spring and has asked me to go with her. Sam at the shop is learning the guitar and a girl I talk to on the high street says she's found the *Santo Daime*.

I should do something I guess. But I have no desire for any of it.

I've done a thousand courses, I've made a thousand resolutions and there are still a thousand things I can't make happen.

This year I've resolved to surf further for cures,
watch a bit more telly,
and not think too hard about anything.

David says I'll know when I'm ready, but that
perhaps it might just do me good,
to catch that early spring.

❖❖❖

WHEN WE wake in the mountains, we lie in our beds, Gratia and me, talking about the rain. We can hear it through the bamboo roof of our small, stone *cassita*, and we watch it through our tiny, square window, like it's a movie just for us. The rain has so many emotions and it's been raining all week in La Gomera.

Gratia says that when she lived here with Ioho Blue, it was always hot this time of year. She remembers driving him round in her bikini and Mercedes Benz, and selling jewellery on the beach to German hippies and people seeking the truth.

Ioho's still so present, here, when we're away from our rituals with Iona and Joe, watching the rainfall.

He would have been seven. It's three years since he died.

Our tiny house is surrounded by mountains, wide-ridged *barancas*, which throw themselves upwards like stairways to heaven. We watch these too, wrapped up in blankets on our balcony, looking up to the gods and back down the waterfalls in an endless game of snakes and ladders.

These mountains show us all their passing thoughts and are constantly changing shape in the mists that come and go and hang around them, smoking.

Sometimes Gratia sees the face of an old *guanche* woman, and I find Japanese hats and the head of a king; but if the clouds come down low, we can't see a thing and it feels like we're part of the sky.

Ioho Blue is laid to rest close by.

A little higher up our mountain, at the *cemetaria*, in its curved white walls of catacombs.

When we went there today, Gratia rushed ahead, and I walked
slowly past the black and white headstones and the drenched
fresh flowers, until I reached them.

He has no headstone: just an open shelf.

The peeling terracotta plaster has the words 'together forever',
carved into it, and the shelf is ablaze with colour.
A picture of dolphins,
a sprig of jasmine,
a plastic toy,
a poem that calls him a heavenly boy.

Amongst the driftwood and shells,
a faded dream-catcher,
a St Maria Guadelupa,
and a painted stone from Ioho's father,
in the colours of the ancestors.
Earth green,
sun yellow,
blood red,
moon blue,
purple for the sky.
The Vesica Pisces Gratia once left close by,
with the symbol of
two worlds joining.

Gratia said she worried when she came here that his things
might be trashed, but they never were. She said there was a
raging storm in La Gomera, the night Ioho Blue was buried, and
that nothing was touched here next morning.

'Even the incense and matches were dry.'

When we were there, I couldn't imagine how it felt for Gratia.
I just lay on the grass while she redesigned his shelf,
and watched a senora in black, arranging white lilies,
for somebody else.

It was when we were walking home,
and I could hear Joe laughing about his concerts, train rides and
childish endeavours,
on the other end of my mobile phone,
that I think I realised,
there was all of life,
and all of death,
between us.

We walked back with our arms round each other, Gratia and I.
The lemon trees were soaking wet and the mountains croaked
with happy frogs.

There was a rainbow over the Valley of the Kings,

and Ioho Blue felt closer than ever.

❖

There are a few thousand miles between the harbour in Gomera
and Cardiff Central, but the distance feels greater when you
travel it at night,
and when you're coming home.

Alex is getting Joe ready for bed when I'm leaving. I speak to him
as I paddle in the clear blue sea. 'I'll be home when you wake
up,' I say. 'I know,' he says to me.

And then I catch a boat, a bus, a plane, and an overnight express
train that tails the break of day,
whistling through the shells of empty stations,
past a million dreaming mothers,
on its way.

I have left my grief behind me on Gomera. I have taken off my

watch and a thin blue line of plaited string hangs loosely round
my wrist now,
like a new horizon.

Time looks more like the sky, the sea;
a reborn mother merging with the girl I used to be.

Coming home, I catch a train,
that's headed back to life again.

❖

Only the flower shops had lights on in my city.

It was early Sunday morning and the clubs had closed as I
walked up from the station to Market Road.
The playgrounds were deserted,
the lazy Taff hummed a song,
'Happy Mothers' Day,' a billboard winked,
like I was special,
the chosen one.

This was my new world.

The boys were still sleeping when I got in. Joe, like a curled up
love spoon in his own bed, and, across the landing, all stretched
out in mine, Alex, Caravaggio dark, in a cloud of white duvet.

They'd left other things to meet me.

There was a trail of star-shaped stickers in the kitchen. The fridge
said that Joe had started to feed himself, with minimal support at
the elbow, the oven that he was doing better with his eyes, and
the microwave pinged that, at the museum, he said the word
dinosaur, clear as a bell.

When I made toast and a cup of tea, the kettle whistled brightly that Eunice, his escort, had taught him to count up to sixty.

On the kitchen table there was an appointment diary left open, covered in ticks, and a paper tree made up of news cuttings, all freshly picked. 'Carers to be called companions', 'disabled actors on TV', branches laced with triumphs over tragedy.

Mark Quinn's statue of Alison Lapper will grace Trafalgar Square and will be12ft high and made of white marble amongst all the bronzed generals there.

There was a card from Alex. It said: 'I could say nice things about you until the cows come home,' with a bunch of cows and 'Welcome Home' inside.
There was a card from Joe which had two giant arms flung open wide, and said: 'This is how I love you'.

Joe woke that day to a brand new mother spooned up beside him on his bed.

'I'm home,' I said.
And when I opened his blind, the sun came up daffodil yellow, and the gardens glistened
like the freshly baptised.

❖ ❖ ❖

WE GROW between things, Joeski and I.
Between the sun and the moon, the earth, winds and sky,
between the places and faces passing by,
we grow like spring,
between a thousand things, Joeski and I.

Between the physio, and the special shoes and the lycra suit, Joe
learns to stand on his own two feet this spring. I watch him in
the school hall at the end of each day, holding on, quite alone,
to a ladder-back chair,
with a smile on his face and the sun in his hair.

Between the teachers, the drivers and Alex and me, his name
is taken off the list for a communication aid, and the speech
therapist finally calls him 'a talker'.

Between the fixing of glasses and the RNIB, he has started to
recognise letters.
And, between a virgin pathway in his brain and the muscles in
his left hand, he can now use a joystick and two buttons to
access the internet. Suddenly he has access to a billion worlds
we never thought he would.

We grow between worlds, Joeski and I, and for every day he
grows in mine, there are countless times I grow in his.

I grow each time he adds more blessings to my tree,
the day we buy his first CD,
and the day we spend hours in the rain
outside Waterstone's
listening to buskers.
I grow when we play popstars, cowboys, kings and queens,
enjoying so much that might never have been.
These days I grow enough to know,
that nothing stays the same for long
and I grow enough to know,

that life is what we make it,
with a child like Joe.

Between the botox appointments for his legs and the plastercasts
on his feet, one pink, one blue, is the day he starts to ride a pony
at a local farm, and between his 'whoa' and 'walk on', I feel my
whole world slow down and look forward to the buttercups.

Between his wheelchair, and his special bike and walking frame,
is the time we grow used to being noticed, and quite enjoy our
certain kind of fame.
Between the free sweets from Sam, and the money the traffic
warden gives him each time she passes, I grow to see all little
acts of pity, as little acts of kindness all the same.

And between the stars and the moon and the sea and the sky,
and the thousands of faces and places passing by.
I know I'll always remember the waiter, who had time to wait
and wait, in that busy restaurant in Cardiff Bay,
for Joe to get his words out,
without once hurrying him,
or even looking in my direction.

And I'll remember the little boy we met at Butlins in half-term.
His is the face in the thousand faces that watched us walk
through the canteen each day, Joe in his bright blue frame by my
side.
The one in that thousand that moved to sit next to us,
the one that offered to carry his pudding,
the one that brought all the other faces closer.

We grow between things
Joeski and I.
Like the spring,
and sometimes I think it's a remarkable thing,
the way humans grow,
and heal,
each other.

❖

It's the week after my birthday that she comes. April.

I'm looking better than before. I've had new clothes for my birthday, gifts of books and perfume – no-one's sent flowers. I've actually been out and bought my own and, for the first time in six years, I've had my hair done.

It was the hairdresser, in fact, that had asked me if I'd see this woman at my kitchen table, and if I didn't already know I wouldn't have guessed she'd been a career woman. She looks a mess.
Tracksuit bottoms and dirty hair;
pale grey eyes that stare into nowhere,
and a baby in her arms, freshly diagnosed.

The hairdresser thought it might help her to talk to me, but I can tell she doesn't really want to. She's already made up her mind not to keep her.

It was a complicated birth, she says. Her daughter lost a minute here, a couple there – and with a husband and two kids at home, she can't afford a complicated life. 'There's only so many times you can shake a rattle and not get a response,' she tells me.

I'm not sure what to say to this woman who doesn't appear to hear me. Her grey eyes look right through me as she rambles on and on about the high-powered career girl she used to be.

She's a go-getter, she says. A certain type of woman who still has plans, and though, of course, she truly admires mothers like me, she could not aspire to do it. She tells me she's read a story that compares life with kids with special needs, to being 'a bit like Holland'. Plodding on, admiring the occasional tulip, while the rest of the world flies past, living it up with the roses. She never was, she says, 'a tulip kind of girl'.

When we're sitting in my kitchen and the flaky sunlight's casting shadows between us on the table, I can see everything in my life

the way this woman's pale grey eyes can see it.
Such a little life, such little victories,
my single parent status
and little kid with special needs,
who'd never get to university.
I can see it in the way she looks at me
that my little colour photos,
in amongst the black and white,
look cheap to her,
like small change.

She is a cloud passing through me.

It's only when she's gone,
and I'm looking in the mirror,
carefully putting my lipstick on,
that the room returns to colour.

❖

On cold and rainy weekend afternoons, I light the fire in Market
Road. When the parks are like wastelands and the jazzy jungles
and cafés are crammed with kids dancing about like time
bombs, we lie down on the floor by our fire, Joeski and I.

We lie on our backs on an old Indian rug, watching the people
rush past the window holding umbrellas and newspapers over
their heads. They're all different shapes and sizes, upside down.

When I lived with Alex I'd never have lit fires on rainy afternoons in May. We'd have found a hundred other things to do.
We used to go to the cinema when it rained and watch films
about love – full of justice and reason and payback – where it
seemed everything worked out. By the time we emerged, the
rain had always stopped and the sun was back out.

Lighting fires has become part of my life now I live with Joe.
Part of the black and part of the blue,
part of the old and the things that we create anew,
between us.
And these firelit days with Joe,
are all I need to know,
that I am more in love
than ever.

Sometimes, by the fire on rainy afternoons, when I'm lying here
watching his eyes drift and wander round the room,
he can bring them to rest on mine,
for seconds at a time,
and I know that
this is the most intimate connection I have ever made,
and that it is possible to make.

I want to call the woman I met in April on these May afternoons,
but she didn't leave a number.

I want to tell her my life with Joe is nothing at all like Holland.

I want her to know that these are not the smaller things.

❖

Usually summer arrives around the back in Market Road, over
the rooftops and along the dry stone walls, slithering in through
the windows like a runaway from somewhere else. Quite sheep-
ish, quite shy, never quite sure whether to come or go – an
altogether quietish affair.

It doesn't this year. It comes round the front, all at once, at half
past twelve on a Friday afternoon and has the touch of a drama
queen about it, a touch of the moment.

Joe is just arriving home, being wheeled across the street,
waving his message book and shouting about the holidays, and
just as he gets here, right at this moment,
the sun pours out its golden heart,
all over our doorstep.

It comes in one personal, floodlit moment, this summer, something just between us, and the two hardy buttercups that have
pushed their way up through a crack in the concrete.

Maybe all summers have something to say, even the quiet ones,
but this one, more than most, talks to me. Walking past the office
girls on lunch break with their skirts rolled up above their knees,
and office boys in windows with their mouths curved down,
walking past the stay-at-homes and shopkeepers in darkened
doorways, I see so many people missing out on things,
all wanting to surrender.

This is the summer I cancel appointments, send back the rocking
chair and cut down on therapies, so that we can feed the birds
instead. The summer the walking, feeding and standing frames
become part of the furniture, part of life, without a flowered
tablecloth in sight. As for the wheelchair, I sometimes wonder
what on earth we'd do without it.

This is the summer Superman defies the impossible by moving
his little finger and the summer the sunflower I planted for Ffion
is at its height.

We get up early to see the sunrise, Joe and I, and eat strawberry
ice cream for breakfast watching the boats bobbing up and
down in Cardiff Bay. I ride my bike again around the parks,
towing him behind me in a carriage with his friend, in and out
of the aspen trees, listening to them laughing loudly.

This is the summer my parents move to a cottage in the country
which has two peacocks, a meadow and a stream and I walk up
and down it in my wellies, towing him behind me in a small blue

dinghy that swirls under the sky. The summer we have picnics with the sheep and the cows and the happy sun.

This is the summer we go to Provence and ride round faster than we should in golf buggies with the wind in our hair, and the summer that Joe hangs out with a gang of kids, who wheel him with them everywhere.

There are times when life feels enough this summer, how it used to feel, when it was silver and nothing was broken,
and there are times, just for moments,
when silver turns gold.

Christine, next door, says it's been 'a run-of-the-mill kind of summer' in Market Road while we've been away. Late flowering, she says. Nothing much has changed.

The sky is milky blue here with the usual goings-on beneath it; Ray pottering in his shed, Elvis drifting out of the window at number 14, Derek passing on his way to the cricket.

There were no miracle cures and no acts of God, as the sun took its course this summer.

Just some gentle reminders of the stuff that makes the world go round,

and a few personal moments of

surrender.

❖

When Joe turns six, I realise that only five of the twenty five who came to his last party, invited him back,
and I realise they're the five that matter,
the five that we like most.

When Joe turns six, he doesn't want to party. He says he wants to go out to a concert wearing his spacesuit, and so we spend the evening mesmerised by *Madame Butterfly*.

There are no fanfares, no Paddy the Clown and no bottles of wine around to drown out sorrow, when Joe turns six.

Life feels good enough to celebrate,

exactly as it is.

❖

I see the counsellor one last time at the end of the summer. He's been away on a course in America, 'getting closer to God'.

I am in the same little room at the back of his house, looking out through the very same window, when he tells me the road trip's over,
and that I have arrived at a place called Acceptance.

When I come back home, I lie on the swing seat in the garden and watch the clouds rush past.

The saxophone student plays tunes I haven't heard before. I think they're his own compositions.

Stronger.

It's like his soul's returned.

year seven

SAM AT the corner shop says it takes ages to accept things. He says he once knew a woman who lost her teenage daughter to cancer and when she finally took her daughter's clothes down to the charity shop, she spent the next six months in cafés, imagining every teenager who passed the window had them on.

It takes time,
and generally I'm doing fine.

Generally I've stopped buying the latest miracle cure, though one day this autumn, as the days are getting shorter I drive 250 miles along the rain-drenched motorways to Cambridge to see a healer off the telly that I've convinced myself is 'top of the range'. My mother comes with me and watches me sign another chunky cheque from Joe's trust fund to the man with the golden Bentley in his drive.

She sang songs on the way home, Joe on her knee in the back – for five and a half hours in the driving rain – and didn't tell me once how foolish I had been.

But, on the whole, I don't do that anymore. These moments are the rare ones now, these are the ones in between.

Generally the weather's fair, more sunny spells than scattered showers, and the more I stop looking for things to happen, the more they seem to come our way. A track for the disabled takes root through the woods at Coed Hills, and the opera house opens in Cardiff Bay, with free, classical concerts on Tuesdays and Thursdays. We spend hours there, Joeski and me, and when we're listening quietly, side by side, life is reaffirmed.

Generally the bad days don't floor me like they used to. Even on rainy days in the café in Pontcanna, we seem to muddle through.

'Mummy I want to walk,' he says, as the children rush about us, and I tell him something about kids that can't see, not half as well as him, and kids that can't hear, not even music, I say, not even a note of it. I tell him some are hungry or poor and others have no parents. 'You're lucky,' I say, 'because you have two that love you, and to be loved is better than anything.'

'But mummy,' he says, looking back to the room. 'I just want to walk.'

My eyes prick small, hard tears like hailstones in the café, but then I find a Milky Way in my pocket and he brightens up and we find something else to do, and the moment is shrunk into a lump in my throat.

Generally I don't cry at all these days and I'm not like the woman Sam knew. I don't get stuck in cafés, I don't look back, and life, it seems, flows on.

Joanna's moved to Stroud where Callum, Jude and Amy run round the rosy apple trees and feed horses at the top of the garden. Julie tells me that Clara does roly-polys and jumping jacks while Freya curls up on the sofa reading Enid Blyton. Gratia says that Iona's starting at the Jal school in Brighton, the first of its kind, where she'll sing and dance, and always be allowed to be that little bit wilder.

My sister's buying a chateau with a swimming pool in France and wants Joe to grace it next summer and, in Chester, William, Lesley, Hari, Lilli and Isabelle clap together furiously as Anna takes her first steps. He sends me the photos on email.

Marchant is made class representative at his mainstream school in Bristol and, in Llanelli, Jac taps out his very first sentence on a computer, using two buttons on either side of his forehead. His mother says she cried when it appeared: 'My name is Jac,' it flickered back: 'I love you mum'.

With all its precious moments, life flows on.

In Cardiff, I sort out the house and tidy up the garden, taking bulging black bags down to the Scope shop on Cowbridge Road.
And when I pass from time to time,
I see a glitter stick, an unused toy or bright red wig,
up on the shelves for two-pounds-fifty,
or one-pound-ninety-nine.

Things are much better than they used to be. I find new things to do – I keep myself busy.

I even go out from time to time
with a businessman called Jamie Divine.

Generally my head is fine,
though my heart retains memories of other things.

❖

Superman dies this autumn.

He had only managed to lift his little finger when he died,
but still, it was enough
to give hope to millions.

❖

My dreams have changed. I don't know why. They're filled with water, filled with sky and people I met only once and thought I had forgotten. The blind man I interviewed in Conwy, who counted the lamp-posts to get home, and the woman in Penmaenmawr, who couldn't have children after several attempts at IVF. I see the details of their faces and all the places where I met them.

Acceptance once seemed like the saddest place to me. A place where people who had fought and lost gave up on miracles.
But as Joe settles into his seventh year in Market Road, he brings another sense of it.

It is October 25 when he swims out of my arms for the very first time.

A clear, crisp day, the leaves are falling and I am standing in a warm pool at a hotel in Cowbridge. Joe, in his orange arm bands, is glued to my chest.

It is as it has always been.
And then suddenly,
it is not.
He swims out of my arms for the very first time.

Moments like this have no sense of time. There is a sudden catch of breath, a sudden sense of weightlessness that runs through the veins.

This is the moment, when I can suddenly play chase with him, just like everyone else does, and I can shout, 'Come back, you're getting away,' just like the regular mums.

But I guess it can never be, for these other mums, what it is to me.
Because this moment,
when this child swims out of my arms for the very first time,
is a rite of passage
to a whole new consciousness.

We lay on our backs in the pool for a while, Joe and I, and closed our eyes. 'Imagine,' I say, 'you are floating in the sea.'

It felt like we were flying.

I think it has changed my dreams, this day. All those aqueous blues with the people I met once, floating, bobbing by.

I hope they also got to know,
Acceptance has its stages
like the sun.

❖

We create our own therapies now, Joeski and me, based round the things he likes to do.

He likes to sing, dance and watch *Strictly Come Dancing* and *The X Factor* on the telly, and so twice a week we just sit side by side, freaking out.

When he dances Joe looks like a tin soldier, the way he moves his arms and legs. His sense of movement has got better.

These days I'm happy with the company I keep.
I am happy when Jamie Divine turns up in his bright blue Porsche, with a dozen red roses, just like the scene from *Pretty Woman*.
And I'm happy when Alex turns up at times he never used to.

Alex says it's like a different place, this house, all neat and tidy.

He likes to have a cup of tea,
and put his feet up on the coffee table.

❖

Joe learns about Jesus in school, and sends some presents to Africa.

He asks if I believe in miracles.

We visit the chapel across the road this Christmas and sit with the congregation, looking up at the beautiful windows, and we look at nativity scenes all over town, and discover just how many baby Jesuses are stolen.

We skate together, him between my legs, on the open-air rink outside the City Hall. We go up on the Ferris Wheel and I point out the lights of the *Western Mail* to him, blinking in the distance.

I squeeze myself on all the baby rides beside him, for the very last time.

There is snow on Christmas Day.

A tsunami hits Asia on Boxing Day, and wipes out entire communities. Everything runs awash with it. The papers are saturated with pictures and there is one of a mother running down a Thai beach, towards certain death, to hold her children.

She is found alive, New Year, the whole of her family safe and well.

'Yes,' I tell him.

For all life's tragedies,

I still believe in miracles.

❖

In the chapel car park across the road, I see a mother that has a baby in her arms with cerebral palsy. I am in the upstairs window and I can't take my eyes off her. She is joining the circle of mothers whose toddlers run about their feet outside the creche and she is trying to talk to them, as his head lolls about on her shoulder.

A bus, full of kids with special needs, passes the window, blocks the view, and when I look again,
the circle has grown wider.

I am looking at mainstream schools again for Joe now. I traipse around them looking for ways that he might fit in, and might possibly be included.

A therapist tells me that children with cerebral palsy can sometimes be treated like the classroom pets or mascots in mainstream. A teacher tells me that the other parents do not like it because they think it holds their kids up. A mother who sent her own son, like Joe, to mainstream, says the first day he came home he asked if she could make him a 'human being'.

A lot of people feel it's best to keep kids separated, but I believe in inclusion,
the way I believe in bigger circles.

❖

At the writing class I join at Chapter, I sit at a large round table with other women, trying to write something.

The teacher brings along a bag of prompts to try to jog our senses.

I am given a doll, which can move its eyes up and down.
'Up is yes, down is no,' I write.

The teacher tells me I have an unusual way of looking at things, but should try perhaps to write a little more!

❖

Acceptance comes in stages
like the sun,
but most of all,
it comes through Joe.

Lately at home he has had a possum, a small button watch he
can now use, to work just about everything. He operates the
lights, the television, the radio and the telephone, and the house
is like a seventies disco. He intercoms me now to talk if we're in
separate rooms.

He's started to use a special fork, which he can bring to his
mouth, unsupported, and a special pencil to make his marks
upon a page. We have discovered now that if we look through
yellow perspex it takes the glare away and he sees things more
clearly.

He's started to direct the taxi drivers to school. 'Turn right at the
end of the road,' he shouts, before he's even left. At school his
teachers say he's started speaking in long sentences, using big
words and is impressing them all with his imaginative stories and
baffling lies.

He's also taken to going out with his 'companions' much more
these days, and has suddenly taken to calling me Nia.

He's started to drive an electric wheelchair.

Lately I feel as if Joe's slowly returning my hands, my eyes, my
arms and legs to me.
Setting me free.

It's him that gives me strength to fight for him forever,
and the strength,
to claim my life back.

❖❖❖

ALEX TAKES photographs of life in the city, and I start to write again – neither of us quite like we used to.

He says that since we've been apart, Joe's taught him to look at life from a 'braver' angle; that he's taught him to see with his heart. Alex sometimes puts on exhibitions now, and people call his photos art.

Now I've begun to write again, I don't want to write in the places I used to. I don't have a desk, or headlines and deadlines in mind, and I drive to the coast, to places I barely know, and write passages.

I go to places where the seagulls squawk and the gorse smells of coconut, and the cliffs are black and bluey-purple on their spine.

I go where the sky feels low enough to touch,
and talks to me of letting go.

I find places I didn't know were part of me,
and write passages that might once have seemed as foreign
as the sky is to the sea.

Joe's changed the way we see things, Alex and I. He's changed the way we think and the kind of places we find meaning.

He's changed the way we grow.

I think we feel things more deeply, Alex and I.

And, sometimes, in the pause of a pen or the click of a shutter, I wonder about the two of us,

and our two little piles
of words and light,
still up there in the attic.

❖

The test at the eye clinic suggests the clarity of vision is now
'good enough to drive a car'. Joe sits on his own, in his wheelchair, matching black and white shapes, the size of peanuts
across the room. It's an exceptional day – he can't always do it
as it seems to come and go – but the doctor says Joe's taught him
some things are possible which he once did not believe were.

He calls him 'an inspiration'.

The psychologist says Joe's doing far better than was ever imagined. This time, when he sits with him at the kitchen table, I
watch Joe pass his test with flying colours. He says Joe's just as
bright as his six-year-old peers, and he'd like to recommend
'full-mainstream' now.

One day this spring when I go to visit Joanna, we walk round
Ruskin Mill, a centre for people with learning difficulties and
look at the beautiful statues and waterfalls they have created.

I have learned this spring,
never to underestimate
children.

❖

The man on the radio says that stem cell research has been
backed in the budget. He says medical science will, almost
certainly, be able to cure the incurable one day.

I don't dwell on medical science these days, too long.

Joe says the grass is rainy,
and I'm sure one day,
he'll be a poet.

I have learned this spring,
to respect life's mysteries,
and to deal in other kinds of magic.

❖

I see things so differently from these mothers I meet in the
mainstream.
I can tell now I've arrived with Joe,
and meet enough this midsummer, to know.

I talk to them in their worlds now. The worlds I thought we'd
never get to, Joe and I. The Beavers in Pontcanna, the local play
centres, his first trial days at 'normal' school.
It's our world now, I guess,
but I can tell by the things that they say,
some don't see it
that way.

There is still a Shadow World.

Some mainstream mothers see us as 'a shame', a tragedy. They
say they don't think they could bring him here and don't think
they could be like me.

They call it 'brave' to be the odd one out. They say that they
couldn't cope and couldn't do what I do; they say they don't
know what, if anything, would pull them through. Mostly, when
they talk to me, they say they 'can't imagine what it's like'.

Alex says people rarely understand the shadow, they forget that
it's part of the light.

These days I don't even see his wheelchair at Beavers, I see the dozen turquoise shirts that surround it. I see him get his badge for helping others, I see him get to carry the flag, I see him take his promise in a group of six year olds that sit quietly, clap and listen as if they've understood his every word.

I don't notice his walking frame down at Riverside play centre. I see a kid called Goodass stop the football in the yard to let him cross. I see each child that waits to hear his name, and see life as the beautiful game.

On his first day in Meadowlane School, I didn't see what the other mother, who gave me a pitying look as we passed the gate, saw. I just saw a child that 'would never do anything,' taking his place in the mainstream.

I saw him join the singing in assembly and the thoughtful African teacher who made him feel at home. I saw the way the kids got closer as the day wore on and how, little by little, the space was conquered in between them.

I learn from the kids how to see things these days.
The things they say, and do
surpass their mothers.

I learn from each and every child around him,
especially the boy with the stud in his ear and the broken shoe,
who just says: 'Hi there, Joe, my name's John.
Look, I wear glasses just like you.'

I see that all kids are different,
I see that all kids are special.

I have started to give talks in schools and colleges and clubs these days about kids like Joe, and I've been writing a book.

Because sometimes, even if just for a moment,
I wish you could imagine

what it's like for me.
Just for a moment
I'd like you to know,

that within the shadow,
there is a constant interference of light.

❖

The pregnant woman at the next till in the supermarket has the whole of a healthy, normal life before her.

It looks like a big balloon up her jumper, all ready for lift off.

I sometimes still have secret wantings,
and I know these wantings,
may never cease.

❖

The gardens in Market Road are in full bloom again. From the window at the back, I can see them all the way along to the corner shop.

I can see the flagpole of Joe's carriage, which Sam stores for me in his back yard, Derek's short-sleeved shirts spinning round on his line and the cats at play in Christine and Ray's.

In our garden, the tree has a blossom of birds and, at its roots, I can see the statue of a mother and a child with a marcasite stone for its head.

Sometimes here it crosses my mind how far we've come, Joe and I. Through our first contact, first hugs, first looks and first words, to these days when he's out playing with all the other children.

It crosses my mind that all my earliest dreams have been fulfilled, and my earliest fears have all been taken care of.

Sometimes here, I wonder at how much he's changed me, and the ways I'm so much stronger than I ever was before. I wonder if, without the common milestones, we have somehow made a thousand tiny steps,
that I appreciate far more.

If, without him, I'd ever have confronted life,
faced fears,
and cared and fought for anything
the way I have for him.
If I could have ever learned
all I've learned through my heartbreak,
and if, without affirming my own spirit,
I would ever have felt this close to god.

Sometimes at this window, I think of all the things that I love more because of Joe, and in this space,
I see our journey as some kind of pilgrimage,
I feel we've found a sacred place.

Standing here a thousand things can cross my mind.
My heart has reshaped a thousand broken pieces,
and, for every moment I still want to heal him,
there are a thousand when I know he's perfect,
exactly as he is.

The most profoundly beautiful, and exquisite, moments I've ever had have been those I've spent with Joe.

And sometimes now it crosses my mind,

that my life is as big and as close as life gets,

and that I am truly,
living it.

❖

I have started to wonder what the city gets up to these days.
What's happening at the paper. I can have my desk back if I
want it.

Life's moving on in Market Road. I've almost written my book,
and the new girl next door will soon be having her baby.
Today I saw the saxophone student at the bus stop on Library
Street. 'He' was a girl after all it seems, just like me!

She had her rucksack and her saxophone case with her, and she
looked like she was leaving town.

I wanted to say something,

but we passed each other by,

without even a word.

❖

The crowd is huge on the last day of term up at Craig-y-Parc. The
whole school gathers for the leavers' assembly, the full range of
teachers and parents and kids from five to eighteen, all squeezed
in tightly amidst a stunning display of mobility aids.

We can't even see Joe, Alex and I. He is somewhere at the back.

The headteacher gives out certificates, shields and the school's
silver cup on the last day of term, and the cheering and clapping
is like a thunderstorm.

It's the same every year.

This year though, there is one difference.

This year, the head says, the cup will not go to the child that's done the best, but to the one that's come the furthest.

This year, he says, this particular child,
has discovered 'independence'.

It is a small, blond-haired boy that emerges from the back of the crowd to get the prize this year. As he weaves his way through, he is smiling and his head is up, and then he sweeps in a cool arc, on to centre stage.

This year it's Joe.

If life so far were a movie or fairytale, it would probably end on our last day of term, this summer.

The details no doubt would be a touch more spectacular, everything healed, restored; no wheelchair perhaps – no doubts about the happy-ever-afters.

But the feeling inside would be the same.

It feels the same as the one, that long-ago summer,
when smiling nurses breezed in and out,
and the sun dropped in through a window,
spellbound.

It feels like a kiss on my belly.

We are still the proudest parents in the world!

❖ ❖ ❖

ON THE window-seat in the front bedroom, I look out on a small patch of postcard-blue sky.

The sun is high; it's mid July.

All's well in Market Road; and I have a sense that a cycle is completed. Joe will be seven at the end of this summer and will start at mainstream school this autumn.

It is one child's lifetime away now, the summer of '98, when we brought a small blue bundle home in our arms, and the only thing to hope for was a miracle from God.

I guess that rare Amazonian flower has not been discovered and the first half of the decade of scientific, medical and technological breakthrough has not brought the cure-all we hoped for.

I guess the world's still pretty much as it was.

Jesus hasn't returned!

But I've learned something of miracles along the way,
and something of this love,
that seems to conquer everything,
in its small achievements of the day.

This love transcends the body
and is a kind of exchange,
this love is all I need to know,
Joe is my miracle.

To understand this love, I guess,
is to understand the light,
sometimes we have to
touch it first.

We plan to take Joe to Disneyland this year, we plan to swim with dolphins, maybe fly in a basket that swings under a big balloon, but after that I can't imagine what the next seven years will hold for us.

I can't imagine what battles he'll have to fight, and what extraordinary gifts he may find in his uncommon life, though I suspect he will fight,
and find…
I think he's like that, Joe,
that kind.

The sky is blue this Friday afternoon. My tree of blessings is littered with small white cards and before I know it the roses will be back in bloom.

Children are gods when they arrive in our arms; we set our hearts by them.

Thank you, Joe,
for everything!

About the Author

Originally from North Wales, Nia Wyn has worked as a journalist in Wales and London. She now lives in Cardiff with her nine-year-old son Joe, where she is studying for an MA in Creative Writing.

All royalties from *Blue Sky July* will go to the Joe Alexander Trust.